The Moving Theatre in association
with Global Uncertainties presents

£2
6/33

THE V

G000069152

The Keepers of Infinite Space

By **Omar El-Khairy**

First performance at Park Theatre:
Wednesday 22 January 2014

THE KEEPERS OF INFINITE SPACE
by Omar El-Khairy

Cast in order of appearance

Saeed	**Edmund Kingsley**
Yael/Sara/Claire	**Laura Prior**
Khalil	**Hilton McRae**
Abner	**John Wark**
Ziv/Tom	**Cornelius Macarthy**
Haneen/Asma	**Sirine Saba**
Tarek/Muhib	**Patrick Toomey**
Shadi	**Philip Correia**

[handwritten: In then Sara 1990, When Khalil escaped.]

The action takes place in Israel and Palestine,
1990 and 2012 - 2014.

The performance lasts approximately 90 minutes.

There will be no interval.

Developer and Director	**Zoe Lafferty**
Designer	**Philip Lindley**
Lighting Designer	**Johanna Town**
Music and Sound Designer	**Richard Hammarton**
Costume Designer	**Susan Kulkarni**
Fight Director	**Tim Klotz**
Executive Producer	**Caroline Rooney**
Producer	**Chris Foxon**
Dramaturg	**Carissa Hope Lynch**
Casting Director	**Emily Jones**
Production Manager	**David Leigh-Pemberton**
Assistant Director	**David Mumeni**
Stage Manager	**Hannah Boustred**
Assistant Stage Managers	**Mica Taylor**
	Bethany Roberts
Assistant Producer	**Jessica Campbell**

We regret there is no admittance or re-admittance to the
auditorium whilst the performance is in progress.

Philip Correia | Shadi

Philip trained at LAMDA.

Theatre includes *The History Boys* (Wyndhams Theatre and National Theatre), *NT50* (National Theatre), *The Pitmen Painters* (National Theatre and Live Theatre), *Hobson's Choice* and *The Syndicate* (Chichester Festival Theatre and Minerva Theatre), *The Merry Wives of Windsor* (RSC), *Northern Odyssey* (Live Theatre Newcastle), *Judgement Day* (The Print Room), *The Cherry Orchard* (Birmingham Rep), *Country Music* (West Yorkshire Playhouse), *Bus Stop* (New Vic/SJT), *Romeo and Juliet* (Jermyn Street Theatre) and *What Cheryl Did Next* (Theatre503).

Television includes *Inspector George Gently*, *Vera*, *Casualty*, *Lewis*, *Hollyoaks*, *Canoe Man*, *Doctors* and *The Bill*.

Film includes *The Hunters*.

Radio includes *Blue Flu*.

Edmund Kingsley | Saeed

Edmund trained at RADA.

Theatre includes *Richard III*, *King John*, *Antony & Cleopatra*, *Julius Caesar*, *The Tempest* and *The Lord Of The Flies* (Royal Shakespeare Company), *The River Line* (Jermyn Street Theatre), *Dangerous Corner* and *The Importance of Being Earnest* (Salisbury Playhouse), *She Stoops to Conquer* (Nottingham Playhouse), *The Duchess of Malfi* and *Volpone* (Greenwich Theatre), *Moscow Live* (HighTide), *Wuthering Heights* (Birmingham Repertory Company), *Rope* (Watermill Theatre), *A Reluctant Hero*, *The Proposal*, *A Christmas Carol* and *As You Like It* (Bridge House Theatre), *'Tis Pity She's a Whore* and *Human Rites* (Southwark Playhouse), *Rosencrantz and Guildenstern are Dead* and *Twelfth Night* (English Touring Theatre), *Julius Caesar* (Menier Chocolate Factory) and *The Taming Of The Shrew* (Thelma Holt National Tour).

Television includes *Breathless*, *Endeavour*, *The Borgias*, *Doctors*, *Sensitive Skin*, *Agatha Christie - A Life in Pictures* and *As If*.

Film includes *Allies*, *Eliza Graves*, *Hugo*, *The Reverend*, *Toto* and *Beast*.

Radio includes *The Christmas Mysteries* and *The Bulldog Has Landed*.

Cornelius Macarthy | Ziv/Tom

Cornelius was born in London and grew up in Sierra Leone. He trained at the Mountview Academy of Theatre Arts.

He recently completed a European tour playing Bertrand Russell, in a production based on Bertrand's life and writings in his book of the same name, directed by multi-award-winning Bosnian director Haris Pašović.

Other theatre includes *Rising Damp* (National Tour), *Antony & Cleopatra* (Chichester Festival Theatre), *1936* (Sadlers Wells), *Come Dancing* (Theatre Royal Stratford East), *12 Proposals for a Better Europe* (Belarus Free Theatre/West Yorkshire Playhouse), *Peter Pan* (York Theatre Royal), *To Kill a Mockingbird* (National Tour), *Welcome to Thebes* (National Theatre), *The Good Soul of Szechuan* (Manchester Library Theatre), *Lost in the Stars* (Queen Elizabeth Hall), *King Cotton* (Manchester Lowry/Liverpool Empire), *A Taste of Honey* (York Theatre Royal), *Ma Rainey's Black Bottom* (Liverpool Playhouse), *One Flew Over the Cuckoo's Nest* (West End), *Lifting the Mask* (National Tour), *Spirit of the Dance* (National Tour), *Cinderella* (Greenwich Theatre), *Drive Ride Walk* (Albany Theatre) and *Notes Across a Small Pond* (Bridewell Theatre).

Television includes *A Touch of Frost*, *Doctors*, *EastEnders*, *Collision*, *Murder Investigation Team*, *Empathy*, *My Hero*, *Torchwood* and *Kingmakers*.

Film includes *Teach Me*, *Candle to Water*, *Patient 17*, *Millions* and *In the Mood*.

Cornelius's world tours with London Community Gospel Choir have led to extensive work as a session singer with a wide variety of recording artists including Blur, Beautiful South, Manu Dibango, Madonna, Celine Dion, Mariah Carey, Tom Jones, Atomic Kitten, Will Young, Billie Piper, R. Kelly, Boy George, Van Morrison and P Diddy.

Hilton McRae | Khalil

Theatre includes *Timon of Athens* (National Theatre), *The Kreutzer Sonata* (Gate Theatre/ La MaMa New York), *End of the Rainbow* (Northampton Theatre Royal), *Experimentum Mundi* (Edinburgh International Festival), *The Oresteia Trilogy* (Fisher Centre, New York), *Rock 'n' Roll* (Manchester Library Theatre), *The Wizard of Oz* (RFH), *Weapons of Happiness* (Finborough Theatre), *Caroline Or Change* (National Theatre), *Rabbit* (West End/Brits off Broadway), *Twelfth Night* (Tour), *The Comedy of Errors* (Sheffield Crucible), *Hamlet* (Northampton Theatre Royal), *The Tempest* (Southwark Playhouse), *Peer Gynt* (Arcola Theatre), *My One and Only* (Chichester Festival Theatre/West End), *Mamma Mia* (West End), *The Front Page* (Donmar Warehouse), *Othello* and *A Doll's House* (Birmingham Rep), *Les Miserables* (West End), *Miss Saigon* (West End), *Hedda Gabler* (Manchester Royal Exchange), *Macbeth* (Dundee Rep), *Les Liaisons Dangereuses* (RSC/Broadway), *The Danton Affair, Troilus and Cressida, As You Like It, Total Eclipse, Piaf, Much Ado About Nothing, The Innocent, Antony and Cleopatra, Captain Swing, The Churchill Play, The Merchant of Venice, Factory Birds* and *Bandits* (RSC) and *LayOff/Yobbo Nowt* (7:84).

Television includes *New Tricks IX, Injustice, Zen, Red Riding Trilogy - 1983, The Execution of Gary Glitter, Lewis, Frances Tuesday, Murder City, Silent Witness, Baby Father, Midsomer Murders, Serious & Organised, Monarch of the Glen, Deacon Brodie, The Justice Game, King of Hearts, First Take, Zorro: The Reward, To Each His Own, William Tell, Roll Over Beethoven, Poppyland, The Kit Curran Radio Show, Forever Young, Leaving* and *Gaskin*.

Film includes *Far From the Madding Crowd, Serena, Power of Three, Stroke of Genius, Mansfield Park, Return of the Jedi, Secret Rapture, Greystoke* and *The French Lieutenant's Woman*.

Laura Prior | Yael/Sara/Claire

Laura trained at Rose Bruford College. Theatre includes *Potholes* (Theatre503), *The Midnight Princess* (Rose Theatre Kingston), *Eisteddfod* (HighTide Festival Theatre for Latitude Festival), *The Comedy of Errors* (Shakespeare's Globe), *Epidemic* (Old Vic New Voices), *Blue Sky/Green Forest* (Arcola Theatre), *The Witch of Edmonton* (Shakespeare's Globe) and *Loyal Women* (Greenwich Theatre).

Sirine Saba | Haneen/Asma

Sirine trained at RADA.

Theatre includes *The Winter's Tale*, *The Taming of the Shrew*, *A Midsummer Night's Dream*, *Twelfth Night* and *HMS Pinafore* (Open Air Theatre, Regent's Park), *The Fear of Breathing* (Finborough Theatre), *Scorched* (Old Vic Tunnels), *Nation* and *Sparkleshark* (National Theatre), *Testing the Echo* (Out of Joint/Tricycle Theatre), *Baghdad Wedding* (Soho Theatre), *Rough Cuts: the Spiral* and *The Rise and Fall of a Lebanese Pop Princess* (Royal Court Theatre), *Midnight's Children*, *Pericles*, *The Tempest*, *The Winter's Tale*, *Beauty and the Beast*, *Tales from Ovid*, *A Warwickshire Testimony* and *A Midsummer Night's Dream* (Royal Shakespeare Company) and *Cinderella* (Bristol Old Vic).

Television includes *Doctors*, *I am Slave*, *Silent Witness*, *Footballers' Wives*, *The Bill* and *Prometheus*.

Film includes *Exhibition*, *Maestro* and *Revolution*.

Sirine has also recorded a wide variety of plays, books and short stories for BBC Radio 3 and BBC Radio 4, including most recently *The Brick*, *The Insider*, *The Reluctant Spy* and *The Deportation Room*.

Patrick Toomey | Tarek/Muhib

Patrick trained at LAMDA.

Theatre includes *Casualties* (Park Theatre), *The Father* (Belgrade Theatre, Coventry), *Lovebirds* (Southwark Playhouse), *Wild Horses* (Theatre503), *On the Waterfront* (Hackney Empire), *Edward II* and *Richard II* (Shakespeare's Globe), *Mister Heracles* (West Yorkshire Playhouse), *The School for Scandal* (Derby Theatre Royal and Northampton Theatre Royal), *Sweet Phoebe* (Hen and Chickens), *The John Wayne Principle* (Nuffield Theatre, Southampton), *The Boys in the Band* (Aldwych Theatre), *The School for Scandal* (English Touring Theatre), *The Recuiting Officer*, *The Merchant of Venice* and *A Midsummer Night's Dream* (Royal Lyceum Theatre, Edinburgh), *The Blue Angel* (Gielgud Theatre), *The Woman in Black* (Fortune Theatre), *The Country Wife* (Holland Park), *Lady Betty* and *As You Like It* (Cheek by Jowl), *A Small Family Business* (Birmingham Rep), *Romeo and Juliet* (London Shakespeare Group), *The Beaux' Stratagem* (Scarborough) and *Pommies* (Warehouse Theatre).

Television includes *Doc Martin*, *The Escape Artist*, *Vera*, *Law and Order UK*, *Missing*, *Mutual Friends*, *Holby City*, *Auf Wiedersehen Pet*,

The Courtroom, Hollyoaks, The Only Boy For Me, The Bill, William and Mary, Monarch of the Glen, Jackson's Wharf, Water Rats, Heartbeat, The House of Angelo, Murder Most Horrid, Annie's Bar, Over Here, Cadfael, The Adventures of Young Indiana Jones, Streetwise and *The Two of Us*.
Film includes *Walking with the Enemy, Balloon Man, The Curse of King Tut's Tomb, Arsene Lupin* and *Pressure Point*.
Radio includes *Soho Nights* and *The Father*.

 **John Wark** | Abner
John trained at RADA.
Theatre includes *Dog in the Manger, Tamar's Revenge* and *Pedro, the Great Pretender* (Royal Shakespeare Company), *Tamburlaine* (Bristol Old Vic and Barbican Theatre), *Nobody Will Ever Forgive Us* (National Theatre of Scotland at the Traverse Theatre, Edinburgh), *The Winter Guest* (Almeida Theatre), *Torch Song Trilogy* (Tron Theatre, Glasgow), *The Only Girl in the World* (Arcola Theatre), *Jamie the Saxt* and *The Fear of Breathing* (Finborough Theatre) and *Thark* (Park Theatre).
Television includes *Robin Hood, Taggart, The Ten Commandments* and *G-Force*.
Film includes *The Fitzroy, A Little Chaos, Breaking the Waves, The Oxford Murders, Late Night Shopping* and *Within the Woods*. John has recently been cast in Werner Herzog's forthcoming film *Queen of the Desert*.

Omar El-Khairy | Playwright
Omar is the Leverhulme Associate Playwright at the Bush Theatre
and co-founder of the international theatre and film collective
Paper Tiger. He is developing a new play *A Soldier Dreams of
White Tulips* as part of Paper Tiger's residency as Associate
Artists at Ovalhouse, where his first full-length play *Sour Lips*
recently premiered. Theatre includes *Return to Sender* (Orange
Tree Theatre), *Given the Times* (Finborough Theatre), *Polling
Booth* (Theatre503), *Eyelids* (Unicorn Theatre), *Lovestrong* (Lyric
Hammersmith), *Burst* (Zoo Venues, Edinburgh Festival), *Longitude*
(The Public Theatre, New York) and *The Arc* (Arcola Theatre). His
short film *No Exit* is in production with Idioms Film in the West
Bank, Palestine, and he is now developing his first feature length
screenplay, *Sheikh*. Omar holds a PhD in Political Sociology from
the LSE.

Zoe Lafferty | Developer and Director
Zoe trained at Drama Centre, London and the Vaktangov Theatre
School, Moscow. Zoe has directed, written and researched
for theatre in Afghanistan, the US, Palestine, Europe and Japan,
and travelled in secret through Syria during the uprising to
collect material for her verbatim play *The Fear of Breathing*. She
is Associate Director of The Freedom Theatre Palestine and
Associate Director and board member of The Red Room Theatre
Company. Directing includes *The Fear of Breathing* (Finborough
Theatre; Akasaka Red Theatre, Tokyo), the world premiere of
Bola Agbaje's *Concrete Jungle* (Riverside Studios), *Gaza: Breathing
Space* (Soho Theatre), *Adult Child/Dead Child* (Unicorn Theatre
and Edinburgh Festival), *Alice in Wonderland* (Freedom Theatre
Palestine) and *Sho Khman?* (Freedom Theatre Palestine and
International Tour). Associate Directing includes *Lost Nation* (The
Red Room). Assistant Directing includes *The Dresser* (Watford
Palace Theatre), *Waiting For Godot* (Freedom Theatre Palestine
and American Tour), *Protozoa* (The Red Room) and *Oikos* (The
Red Room). Zoe co-wrote *Off Record* with Paul Wood, a verbatim
piece on the Israel/Palestine conflict performed at the Soho
Theatre, and has developed work with National Theatre Wales.

Philip Lindley | Designer
At the Finborough Theatre, Philip is Associate Designer, and has
designed *Mirror Teeth*, *Drama At Inish*, *Autumn Fire*, *The American
Clock*, *Merrie England*, *The Fear of Breathing*, *Passing By*, *Somersaults*,

Rooms and *As Is*. Trained as an architect, Philip began his theatre career as a set and lighting designer before joining the BBC TV Design Department. During 25 years at the BBC, he worked on every type of production including *Dr. Who, Blackadder, Top Of The Pops, Mastermind, Swap Shop, Play For Today, Play For Tomorrow, 30 Minute Theatre, Lorna Doone, Z For Zacharias, The Tripods, Juliet Bravo, Rings On Their Fingers, The Kamikaze Ground Staff Dinner Party, Goodbye Darling, Tomorrow's World*, the 1981 Royal Wedding and *The Scientist*. After leaving the BBC, he worked as a freelance theatre consultant before moving to Lisbon where he continued to design sets and lighting for Portuguese theatre including productions of *Cymbeline, Saturday Sunday Monday, The Bear, The Proposal, Recklessness, Tone Clusters, One For The Road, A Time For Farewells* and *Dracula*. Since returning to live in the UK, he has designed *Nerve, The Good Doctor* and *Sleeping Dogs* (Baron's Court Theatre), *Miss Julie* (Theatro Technis), *The Three Sisters* and *Endgame* (Bridewell Theatre), *Fair Em* and *Measure For Measure* (Union Theatre), *The Theban Plays* (The Scoop – Time Out best free London event of 2013) and *Passing By* (Tristan Bates Theatre).

Johanna Town | Lighting Designer
Theatre includes *What the Butler Saw, Some Like It Hip Hop, Betrayal, Speaking in Tongues, Fat Pig, Hello and Goodbye, Top Girls, Via Dolorosa* and *Beautiful Thing* (West End), *Haunted* (New York, Royal Exchange and Sydney Opera House), *Rose* (National Theatre and Broadway), *My Name is Rachel Corrie* (Royal Court Theatre, West End and New York), *Guantanamo* (New York, Tricycle Theatre and West End), *Arabian Nights* and *Our Lady of Sligo* (New York), *The Steward of Christendom* (Out of Joint, Broadway and Sydney), *Macbeth* (Out of Joint, World Tour and Arcola Theatre) and *The Permanent Way* (Out of Joint, National Theatre and Sydney). Johanna is an Associate Artist for Theatre503 where recent productions include *The Life of Stuff, Man in the Middle, The Final Shot* and *Ship of Fools*. Her many other theatre credits include *Fences* (Theatre Royal Bath), *Smack Family Robinson* (Rose Theatre, Kingston), *Straight* (Bush Theatre and Crucible Theatre, Sheffield), *Medea, Romeo and Juliet* (Headlong), *Moon on A Rainbow Shawl* (National Theatre), *The Wind in the Willows* (Polka Theatre), *Blue Heart Afternoon* and *Lay Down Your Cross* (Hampstead Theatre), *Llywyth* (Sherman Cymru and Theatr Genedlaethol Cymru), *Charged* (Soho Theatre), *Miss Julie, Private Lives, The Glass Menagerie* and *A Raisin in the Sun* (Royal Exchange Theatre,

Manchester) and *The Tragedy of Thomas Hobbes* (RSC).
Johanna has also worked extensively at the Royal Court Theatre
where her credits include *Rhinoceros*, *The Arsonists* and *My Child*. She
has also lit numerous productions for Out Of Joint including *Our
Country's Good*, *Bang Bang Bang*, *Dreams of Violence*, *Our Lady of Sligo*,
The Permanent Way and *King of Hearts*.
Opera includes *Carmen*, *Kátya Kabanová*, *Cinderella*, *Phaedra & Ariadne
Auf Naxos* and *The Secret Marriage* (Scottish Opera), *The Marriage
of Figaro* for Classical Opera Company and *Tobias and the Angel* for
Almeida Opera Festival.

Richard Hammarton | Music and Sound Designer
Theatre includes *Sizwe Bansi is Dead* and *Six Characters Looking
for an Author* (The Young Vic), *The Mountaintop* (Theatre503 and
Trafalgar Studios), *The Taming of the Shrew* (Shakespeare's Globe),
Brilliant Adventures, *Edward II* and *Dr Faustus* (Royal Exchange Theatre,
Manchester), *Speaking in Tongues* (Duke of York's Theatre), *A Raisin
in the Sun* (Lyric Theatre Hammersmith, and National Tour), *I Know
How I Feel About Eve* (Hampstead Theatre), *The Last Summer* (Gate
Theatre, Dublin), *Mudlarks* (HighTide Festival, Theatre503 and Bush
Theatre), *Ghosts* (Duchess Theatre), *The Pitchfork Disney* (Arcola
Theatre), *Judgement Day* (The Print Room), *Same Same, Little Baby
Jesus* and *Fixer* (Ovalhouse), *Cheese* (Fanshen Theatre), *An Inspector
Calls* (Theatre by the Lake, Keswick), *What Happens in the Winter*
(Upswing), *Persuasion*, *The Constant Wife*, *Les Liaisons Dangereuses*,
Arsenic and Old Lace, *The Real Thing* and *People at Sea* (Salisbury
Playhouse), *Platform* (Old Vic Tunnels), *Pride and Prejudice* (Theatre
Royal Bath and National Tour), *The Shooky*, *Steve Nallon's Christmas
Carol* and *Dealer's Choice* (Birmingham Rep), *Hello and Goodbye*
and *Some Kind of Bliss* (Trafalgar Studios), *Breakfast with Mugabe*
(Theatre Royal Bath), *Someone Who'll Watch Over Me* (Theatre Royal
Northampton), *Inches Apart*, *Ship of Fools*, *Natural Selection* and *Salt
Meets Wound* (Theatre503) and *Blowing* (National Tour).
Film includes *The Pier*, *First the Worst*, *A Neutral Corner*, *Snow*, *The
Button* and *Raptured*.
Television includes *Agatha Christie's Marple*, *No Win No Fee*, *Sex 'N'
Death*, *Wipeout*, *The Ship*, *Konigsspitz*, *K2* and *The Fisherman's Wife*.
Orchestration includes *Agatha Christie's Marple*, *Primeval*, *Dracula*,
Jericho, *If I Had You*, *A History of Britain*, *Silent Witness*, *Dalziel and
Pascoe*, *Alice Through the Looking Glass*, *The Nine Lives of Tomas Katz*
and *Scenes of a Sexual Nature*.
Interactive work includes pieces at the Foundling Museum, *Moore
Outside* at Tate Britain, *You Shall Go to the Ball* at Royal Opera House
and *Light* at BAC.

Susan Kulkarni | Costume Designer

Susan trained at Somerville College, Oxford University, and RADA.

Theatre includes *Detroit, Cesario, More Light, The Prince of Denmark* and *King James' Bible* (National Theatre), *Herding Cats* (Hampstead Theatre), *And Darkness Descended* (Punchdrunk), *I Didn't Always Live Here* (Finborough Theatre) and *The Prince and the Pauper* and *The Legend of Captain Crow* (Unicorn Theatre), *Narrative* (Royal Court Theatre), *Zombie Lab* (The Science Museum), *Measure for Measure* and *Marat/Sade* (RSC) and *The Look Out* (Royal Festival Hall).

Susan is currently Head of Costume for Future Cinema and Secret Cinema and she designs all of their large-scale immersive productions. Her work includes *The Shawshank Redemption, Brazil, Blade Runner, Prometheus, The Red Shoes, One Flew Over the Cuckoo's Nest* and the interactive premiere of *Watchmen*.

Television/Film credits include *Downton Abbey II, Dancing on the Edge* by Stephen Poliakoff, *Mrs Dickens' Family Christmas, Big Ballet, Eye and Mermaid* and *Three* and *A Dream* (shorts shot in Qatar for the Doha Film Institute).

Advertisements include *Push, PETA* and *Peroni.*

Tim Klotz | Fight Director

Tim has been a fight director for almost twenty years and has been resident fight director for the Drama Centre London since 2004. He has worked at Shakespeare's Globe, Lyric Hammersmith, Gate Theatre, Nashville Ballet, Royal Festival Hall, Sony, SEGA, Rebellion and a host of smaller theatres and educational projects. Tim was on the staff of the Paddy Crean International Stage Combat Conference in Banff, Canada.

Caroline Rooney | Executive Producer

Caroline is a Global Uncertainties Leadership Fellow and Professor of African and Middle Eastern Studies at the University of Kent. Her research by practice engages with arts activism and popular culture towards coming to terms with a new Middle East in the making. Theatre includes *The Rebel Cell* at El Sawy Culturewheel in Cairo.

Film includes *The Road to Midan Tahrir*, featuring interviews she carried out with Egyptian writers in 2010. Caroline's poetry appears in an anthology of human rights poetry (London Human Rights Consortium, 2013) and she has published widely on the Arab avant-garde and popular culture, liberation struggles and their aftermaths, and alternative enlightenments. With director Mai Masri she is currently working on a documentary film addressing the experiences of Palestinian child prisoners. Her current research programme is entitled: *Imagining the Common Ground*.

Chris Foxon | Producer

Chris read English at Oxford University and trained at the Royal Central School of Speech and Drama on an AHRC Scholarship. Chris is the producer of the multi-award-winning Papatango Theatre Company and was an assessor for the 2013 T.S. Eliot Commissions with the Old Vic Theatre.

Productions include *Happy New* (Trafalgar Studios), *The Fear of Breathing* (Finborough Theatre and Akasaka Red Theatre, Tokyo), *Unscorched* and *Pack* for Papatango Theatre Company at the Finborough Theatre, *Old Vic New Voices 24 Hour Plays* (The Old Vic), *The Madness of George III* (Oxford Playhouse) and *Tejas Verdes* (Edinburgh Festival).

Theatre as Assistant Producer includes *On The Threshing Floor* (Hampstead Theatre), 'Endless Poem' as part of *Rio Occupation London* (BAC, People's Palace Projects and HighTide Festival Theatre) and *Mudlarks* (HighTide Festival Theatre, Theatre503 and Bush Theatre).

Carissa Hope Lynch | Dramaturg

Carissa trained at the University of California and Royal Central School of Speech and Drama.

As a dramaturg, theatre includes *Gastronauts* (Royal Court, Theatre Upstairs), *Peckham: the Soap Opera* (Royal Court, Bussey Building and Theatre Upstairs), *Reasons to be Cheerful* (Theatre Royal Stratford East, New Wolsey, National Tour), *Prometheus Awakes* (Greenwich and Docklands International Festival), *The Garden* (London 2012 Festival), and *The Iron Man* (Brighton Festival, GDiF). She supported script and concept development in respective collaborations between Graeae and the Royal Shakespeare Company, Theatre Royal Plymouth, and Dundee Repertory. Carissa has read for the Bruntwood Prize for playwriting and the Verity Bargate Award, and she is the Deputy Literary Manager at the Royal Court Theatre.

Emily Jones | Casting Director

Theatre includes *Unscorched* (Papatango Theatre Company at the Finborough Theatre), *As You Like It* and *Richard III* (Changeling Theatre) and *World Enough and Time* (Dalston Bunker).

Theatre as assistant to Ginny Schiller includes *1984* (Headlong), *Relative Values* (Theatre Royal Bath), *Scenes from a Marriage* (St James Theatre), *A Day in the Death of Joe Egg* and *Ghosts* (Rose Theatre Kingston) and *Pride and Prejudice* (Open Air Theatre, Regent's Park).

Film includes *Limbo* and *Ibiza Undead*.

David Leigh-Pemberton | Production Manager

David trained at Guildhall School of Music and Drama and is a freelance general manager and production manager.

Production management includes *Journeying Boys* (Guildhall School of Music and Drama), *Nothing is the End of the World (Except the End of the World)*, *Somersaults* and *Events While Guarding the Bofors Gun* (Finborough Theatre).

David was Production Assistant on *Potted Potter* (Garrick Theatre) and General Manager for *Sunstroke* (Platform Studio Theatre). David is Technical Manager for the annual charity event *West End Bares* (Café De Paris).

David Mumeni | Assistant Director

David trained as an actor at Drama Centre, London and is an Associate Artist of The National Youth Theatre.

Theatre as an actor includes *'Tis Pity She's a Whore* (Cheek by Jowl), *Product Placement* (Nabokov) and *The Machine* (The Donmar Warehouse and New York).

Television as an actor includes *Fresh Meat*, *PhoneShop*, *Cuckoo*, *Confessions From The Underground* and *Whitechapel*.

Film as an actor includes *The Inbetweeners Movie* and *Noble*.

Writing includes *Our Days of Rage* (Old Vic Tunnels) and *My Christian Name* (The Lantern Theatre, Liverpool).

Directing includes *Odd Ball* (Lost Theatre) and *Fishbowl* (Not Too Tame).

Assistant Directing includes *Lysistrata* and *Poundtown* (Greenwich Theatre).

Jessica Campbell | Assistant Producer
Jessica read English at Oxford University.
Theatre as producer includes *Hansel and Gretel* (Opera in Space at the Bussey Building), *Bloody Poetry* (Keble O'Reilly Theatre) and *Mephisto* (Oxford Playhouse), which transferred to the International Student Drama Festival 2013, *The State Vs John Hayes* (Hen and Chickens Theatre and Edinburgh Festival) and *The Comedy of Errors* (Southwark Playhouse, Yvonne Arnaud Theatre, Guildford, and the Tokyo Metropolitan Theatre, Japan).

Production Acknowledgements
Production Photography | **Richard Davenport**
Production Artwork | **Nidal El-Khairy**
Graphic Design | **Felix Trench**

This production was initiated by Caroline Rooney in dialogue with Mai Masri as part of the RCUK funded *Imagining the Common Ground* programme. The play was inspired by true stories and developed through research by Caroline Rooney and Zoe Lafferty. We would like to thank the following people and organisations in Palestine for their help and support: the YMCA in Beit Sahour and Al-Khalil and the young ex-prisoners we met through them; Addameer; the Abu Jihad Museum; Zakaria Zubeidi, Faisal Abu Alhayjaa, Majd Beltaji, Momin Switat and Adnan Torokman.

The play was initially developed with the following actors: Nyasha Hatendi, Nicholas Karimi, Siân Polhill-Thomas and John Wark.

We would also like to thank the following:
Henry Gilbert, Micheal Cusick, Nadia Nadif, Zoë Nicole, Abram Rooney, Sian Goff, Miles Mitchell, Paul Mclaughlin, Lola Frears, Nick Bruckman, Anna Brooks-Beckman, Rodrigo Penalosa Pita, Richard Listor, Hannah Jenner, Bérengère Auriaudo De Castelli, Anastasiya Trayanova, Rita Sakr and Julia Borossa.

About Park Theatre

"A spanking new five-star neighbourhood theatre"
Independent

Opened in May 2013, Park Theatre consists of two theatres — with 200 seats and 90 seats respectively — plus a dedicated community learning space, an all day cafe-bar and ancillary facilities.

With a broad artistic policy encompassing both classics and new writing and an ambitious outreach programme, Park Theatre sits at the heart of its community.

"A first-rate new theatre in north London"
Daily Telegraph

Park Theatre is a registered charity (number 1137223) and receives no public subsidy. Ticket sales alone are not enough to cover the running costs and it is only through your support that we can keep the theatre thriving.

We rely on their tremendous support of our volunteer ushers to help staff the building — and enjoy including them in the Park family. If you're local and would like to volunteer as an usher then we'd love to hear from you. Please email our Front of House Manager on foh@parktheatre.co.uk

If you're able to support us financially there are many ways from donating just £1 with your ticket booking to becoming a friend, naming a seat and even legacy giving — many of these come with an exciting array of benefits including priority booking, private tours and receptions. To discuss how you can support us please email our Development Director on development@parktheatre.co.uk

For more information and the latest on upcoming shows please visit the website: parktheatre.co.uk

We look forward to seeing you again soon.

Very best wishes,

Jez Bond, Artistic Director

A note on the Israeli prison system in Palestine

On 7 June 1967, the Israeli Occupying Forces issued Military Proclamation No. 1, which stated that all legal authority over the occupied Palestinian territory would fall in the hands of the Israeli military commander in the "interests of security and public order".

Since then, the Israeli military authorities have issued more than 3,000 military orders, which have been used to detain over 800,000 Palestinians, representing approximately 20% of the Palestinian population and as much as 40% of the male Palestinian population. Since the beginning of the second intifada, more than 50,000 Palestinians have been arrested.

After interrogation, Palestinians arrested by the IOF may be released, or charged and prosecuted through Israeli military courts, or placed in administrative detention, a form of detention without charge or trial.

All but one of the prisons where Israel detains Palestinian prisoners are located inside Israel, in direct contravention of Article 76 of the Fourth Geneva Convention, which states that an Occupying Power must detain residents of occupied territory in prisons inside the occupied territory. In addition to illegality under international law, the practical consequence of this system is that many prisoners have difficulty meeting with Palestinian defence counsel and do not receive family visits, as their attorneys and relatives are denied permits to enter Israel on "security grounds".

On the date this went to press 4996 Palestinians are being held in Israeli prisons, including 159 children.

Please see www.addameer.org for further information.

THE KEEPERS OF INFINITE SPACE

Omar El-Khairy

THE KEEPERS OF INFINITE SPACE

OBERON BOOKS
LONDON

WWW.OBERONBOOKS.COM

First published in 2014 by Oberon Books Ltd
521 Caledonian Road, London N7 9RH
Tel: +44 (0) 20 7607 3637 / Fax: +44 (0) 20 7607 3629
e-mail: info@oberonbooks.com
www.oberonbooks.com

A catalogue record for this book is available from the British
Library.

PB ISBN: 978-1-78319-076-8
E ISBN: 978-1-78319-575-6

Cover illustration by Nidal El-Khairy
Cover design by Felix Trench

Printed, bound and converted
by CPI Group (UK) Ltd, Croydon, CR0 4YY.

For my family – scattered across the globe

In loving memory of Emile Habiby

Characters
in order of appearance

KHALIL, *thirty-three-year-old Palestinian resistance fighter / fifty-five-year-old businessman and property developer*

SAEED, *twenty-eight-year-old Palestinian bookseller*

YAEL, *twenty-four-year-old Israeli prison guard*

ABNER, *forty-five-year-old Israeli Defence Force Captain*

ZIV, *twenty-year-old Israeli (Ethiopian) prison guard*

SARA, *twenty-six-year-old Israeli army doctor*

TAREK, *thirty-year-old Palestinian spy*

HANEEN, *twenty-six-year-old Palestinian secondary school teacher*

MUHIB, *thirty-four-year-old Palestinian resistance fighter / fifty-six-year-old Palestinian prisoner*

SHADI, *sixteen-year-old Palestinian prisoner*

TOM, *twenty-five-year-old British International Committee of the Red Cross aid worker*

CLAIRE, *twenty-six-year-old British journalist*

ASMA, *twenty-four-year-old Palestinian student*

BEAT: less than denoted in text.

A dash (–) denotes an interruption
or change in thought/intention in dialogue.

A forward slash (/) denotes an interruption
by another character so that lines might overlap.

An asterix (*) denotes whole lines spoken simultaneously.

An ellipses […] denotes a silent but distinct response.

Setting

Israel/Palestine. 1990 & 2012

Acknowledgements

To Nidal El-Khairy, for creating such a boom image, Madani Younis, Omar Elerian and the rest of the Bush family, Jessica Cooper, Kat Buckle, Khaled Ziada, Mohanad Yaqubi and the whole Palestine Festival of Literature crew – especially Omar Robert Hamilton, Yasmin El-Rifae, Ahdaf Soueif and China Miéville – for the truly inspiring week we spent together roaming across historical Palestine.

Author's Note

Considering both the current climate of British political theatre-making and the particular world of this play, I feel it's important to reiterate that there's no simple message at the heart of this piece – its intention is not to educate, but rather to move and inspire. Moreover, it wasn't penned solely in the hope of recreating the lived experience of Palestinians incarcerated in Israeli prisons – its creation was as much the act of the heart and imagination.

Therefore, I wholeheartedly encourage and celebrate any urge on behalf of the director and/or actors to steer away from the trappings of naturalism and embrace the full spirit of the piece.

25

This question floored me. But he had calmed down and now he came closer to me and patted me on the shoulder in a fatherly manner: 'Now let this be a lesson to you. You should realise that we have the latest equipment with which to monitor your every movement, even including what you whisper in your dreams. With our modern apparatus we know all that happens, both within the state and outside it. Take care you don't ever behave this way again.'

I responded merely by continuing my violent shaking, repeating only, 'I am an ass! I am an ass!'

I kept this up till he left, after he had finally removed his sunglasses. Then I began invoking God's mercy on my father's soul, for he had been the first person to discover what an ass I am.

– Emile Habiby *The Secret Life of Saeed: The Pessoptimist*

The Company should be present as the audience enters and remain on stage for the duration of the performance.

REDEVELOPMENT

Morning.

Conference room.

KHALIL   Welcome – and thank you all for being with us today. I'm aware that last night's troubles have made getting here near-impossible, but we appreciate your resoluteness. It's an absolute pleasure to welcome internationals to see our showroom and witness the latest development phase of Rawabi. It's days like today that remind us all of what we're striving for. Rawabi – meaning 'the hills' – is a cutting-edge development project and the first Palestinian planned city, with homes for over 40,000 residents. As you can see, it's being built across two glistening hilltops – just two kilometers from here. Costing in the region of $850 million, it will be conveniently situated at the heart of Palestine – 9 km from Ramallah, 25 km from Jerusalem and Nablus, 40 km from Tel Aviv and 70 km from Amman. This new city will be strategically positioned for regional access, sitting squarely at the global gateway to the Middle East for both the North American and European markets. It will be both the largest construction project and the biggest private foreign direct investment ever made in the Palestinian territories. Our unique vision will ultimately make it a home for all Palestinians, as well as a desirable travel destination for internationals like yourselves.

HOME SWEET HOME

Late night.

Israeli military holding station.

Holding cell.

A bucket full of dirty water.

SAEED is in a stress position – he is blindfolded, crouched with his hands behind his back, with both his forehead and knees against the wall.

YAEL is stood in the corner.

SAEED	I haven't done anything.
	Please.
	What do you want from me?
	(Beat.) I need /
YAEL	/ I said crouch, knees, head, wall – and don't move.

Pause.

SAEED	Water.
YAEL	[…]
SAEED	Can I – please.
YAEL	[…]
SAEED	Just a sip.
	Something to /
YAEL	/ Hands on head.
SAEED	[…]
YAEL	*(Beat.)* You want something to drink?
SAEED	Yes.
YAEL	Then.

Pause.

SAEED raises his cuffed hands gingerly on his head.

YAEL	Good.
SAEED	Please.
YAEL	Some water?
SAEED	*(Turning around hesitantly.)* Yes – yes.

YAEL takes the bucket and throws the dirty water over SAEED.

BEGINNINGS

Interrogation room.
SAEED is shackled to a chair.
YAEL and ZIV are stood behind SAEED – facing ABNER.
ABNER watches on in silence.

SAEED	Where am I?
	(Beat.) (Shouting.) Where am I?
	(Shouting.) Hey.
	(Shouting.) Hey – hey, answer me.

Pause.

SAEED	*(Beat.)* Please.
	Just tell me – please.

ABNER nods.

YAEL	On the moon.
ZIV	[…]
SAEED	The moon.
	(Laughing.) (Beat.) I'm on the moon.
ZIV	[…]
YAEL	*(Looking at ZIV.)* In a submarine.
ZIV	[…]

ABNER looks at ZIV.

ZIV	In –
	In –
YAEL	*(Beat.)* In Honolulu.
ZIV	[…]
YAEL	On the Galapagos Islands.
	Inside the belly of a whale.
	At the Pyramids in Giza.
	On top of the Empire State Building.

Pause.

YAEL   Do you know how much the Earth weighs?

SAEED   […]

YAEL   Approximately.
                       Go on – take an educated guess.

SAEED   […]

A NEW LIFE

Conference room.

KHALIL   The project was inspired by what we saw as the dramatic impact real estate was having on the economy and its potential to create jobs fast. It's a public-private partnership and is jointly funded by a Palestinian businessman, with investment from both Qatar and the Palestinian National Authority. However, with the continued military occupation, we, as a people, have grown reliant on international aid. But we believe that with projects such as Rawabi, we can start to achieve economic independence and begin shaping our own future.

Pause.

KHALIL   *(Beat.)* So let me now introduce you all to our latest development phase. The city centre model has a new, unique character. It will focus on job creation – particularly in the creative industries. It will concentrate on the provision of real life experiences for visitors, shoppers, and for those who are interested in gaining strategic advantages for their businesses. We are also in the process of finalising plans for a five-star superior hotel.

Pause.

KHALIL   I'm sorry.

                Excuse me for a moment.

SIGNING IN

Interrogation room.

YAEL shackles SAEED to a chair.

ZIV is stood beside YAEL.

YAEL   Stop staring at me.

SAEED   [...]

YAEL   Did you hear what I said?

SAEED   [...]

ZIV   Shouldn't we – you know?

YAEL   No.

ZIV   But they're definitely too tight on him.

YAEL   *(Beat.)* What's your name again?

ZIV   Ziv.

YAEL   Ziv?

ZIV   Yes.

YAEL   Odd name that – Ziv.

ZIV   [...]

YAEL   It's your first day, isn't it?

ZIV   Yes.

YAEL   Then learn your place and shut your mouth.

ZIV   [...]

        ABNER enters – and watches on.

YAEL   *(To SAEED.)* You're still doing it.

SAEED   I'm not.

YAEL   I saw you – looking at me like that.
                (Beat.) Perv.

SAEED   You're lying.

Beatrys' left out.

YAEL	You were looking at me the way a teenager would – like you'd never seen a woman before.
	You're not used to seeing women in control, are you?
	(Beat.) How does that make you feel?
SAEED	You don't know what you're taking about.
YAEL	Such a sexually frustrated lot you are – you don't get to see much skin, do you?
	(Beat.) You want to see some skin?
SAEED	[…]
YAEL	Well, do you?
SAEED	[…]
ABNER	I don't blame you myself.
	I mean, you shouldn't feel guilty – we've all thought it.
	(Beat.) Look at her. She's hot.
	(Beat.) Do you know she once made the cover of *Maxim*?
	What was the feature spread again?
YAEL	Women of the Israeli Defence Forces.
ABNER	That's it.
	(Beat.) And that caption –
YAEL	She can jump out of an airplane without so much as getting her makeup smeared. That takes skill.
ABNER	A hundred percent true – I tell you.
	She shines over all of us.
	She can kick your ass too – and you might even like it.
Pause.	
ABNER	*(Beat.)* But you're not interested in all that. You're a cultured man, aren't you? A man of words. *(Beat.)* Saeed Shaka.

SAEED	Why are you holding me here?
ABNER	First tell us about this bookshop of yours. The one on Omar Ibn Al-Khattab Street.
SAEED	There's nothing to tell.
ABNER	Nothing? Really? *(Beat.)* But we already know all about it – what you get up to in there.
SAEED	What I get up to? I sell books.
ABNER	And who do you fraternise with?
SAEED	No one.
ABNER	That's not what our intelligence agencies suggest. They have it marked down as a hotbed of subversive activities.
SAEED	This is crazy.
ABNER	*(Beat.)* What do you think your father would make of all of this?
SAEED	My father?
ABNER	Some people say they're useless, arcane objects – books. *(Beat.)* Did they stop the Indonesian tsunami, they ask. *(Beat.)* Or the bombings of Hiroshima and Nagasaki. You want to philosophise with the roof rotting over you, they say. Waiting for it to cave in over your family's head. To rot – but to be free all the same. *(Beat.)* Well, what does one say to that?
SAEED	Nothing.
ABNER	Nothing. Right. But we both know that books still possess a power – an unquantifiable power of persuasion. *(Beat.)* Am I right?

SAEED	[...]
ABNER	You don't fool me, Saeed.
	(To ZIV.) (Beat.) Read him his rights.
ZIV	Yes, sir.
ZIV	*(Struggling to read.)* One. You have the right to remain –

Pause.

ABNER	What's the matter?
ZIV	Nothing, sir.
ABNER	Then read it out – clearly.
ZIV	Yes, sir.
	(Beat.) Two. You /
ABNER	/ No. From the beginning.
ZIV	*(Beat.)* Do you want me to walk in again?
ABNER	No, you idiot. Just read.
ZIV	One. You have the right to remain silent. Two. You have the right to –
	(Pause.)
ABNER	Can't you read Hebrew?
ZIV	[...]
ABNER	*(Beat.)* Where are you from?
ZIV	Tigray Province – Ethiopia, sir.
	(Beat.) But this is my home now.
ABNER	[...]
ZIV	*(Beat.)* Do you want me to finish reading, sir?
ABNER	No.
	(To SAEED.) (Beat.) Just sign.

FOR SALE

KHALIL	I'm sorry about that. *(Beat.)* As I was saying, our focus now is on creating three to five thousand jobs in the city itself for potential

businesses and young entrepreneurs. And
with over 600 units already sold, we intend
to reach our goals by the end of the year
– where people move in and we see them
living happily, enjoying the Rawabi life.

Pause.

KHALIL   Sorry – I just lost my –
Bare with me.

Pause.

KHALIL   Thousands of people have visited already –
including U.S. Senator John Kerry, USAID
Mission Director, David Harden and Senior
Advisor to the American Special Envoy to
the Middle East, George Mitchell. But it's not
only the officials. It's internationals who have
come here – particularly Jews who lobby in
Israel. We want to show them that we're not
about destroying Israel, we're about building
Palestine. We're about having a better life
for ourselves and our people. They prefer to
see a prosperous Palestinian state, because a
prosperous Palestinian state is also good for
them and their beloved –

Pause.

KHALIL   *(Beat.)* Could we just stop, please.
(Beat.) I'm sorry.
My son – he was arrested last night.

TIME

ABNER   Charge unknown.

YAEL / ZIV   Administrative detention.

Pause.

SAEED   Forty days.

TURN IT UP

Holding cell.

SAEED is wearing large over-ear headphones. He is blindfolded.

Barney & Friends ending song 'I Love You' blares out – it's painfully loud.

ZIV is stood in the corner.

Long pause.

ZIV   […]

> *Long pause.*
>
> *ZIV's discomfort begins to surface.*
>
> *Pause.*

                    No –

> *Pause.*

                    I can't –

> *Pause.*

                    (Beat.) I can't do this.

> *ZIV rips the headphones off SAEED.*

SAEED   […]

> *ZIV takes a deep breath – and a long exhale.*
>
> *Pause.*

SAEED   *(Beat.)* It's all gone quiet – as if the world's just died.

ZIV   […]

ONLY FOR A SECOND

Outside the holding cell.

ABNER   I think so that you don't have to.

ZIV   […]

ABNER   In its natural state, a man's skin is far too thin for this world. *(Beat.)* And that's why men try so hard to thicken it – the only way they know how.

(Beat.) Do you understand?

ZIV	Yes, sir.
ABNER	*(Beat.)* Come here.
ZIV	[...]
ABNER	Did you hear me?

ZIV moves closer.

ABNER	Are you a coward?
ZIV	No, sir.
ABNER	Bullshit.
	After everything this country has done to take your people in over the years.
	Show some fucking gratitude.
ZIV	I do, sir.
	I'm thankful to be here.
	Many have died trying to get out – to get here and be part of the land of Israel.
	But I'm strong because of my religion – my faith.
ABNER	And we have afforded you this exceptional opportunity.
ZIV	Sir.
	After the revolution, relatives of mine were some of those traded by Colonel Mengistu for arms from here – two hundred people airlifted on an Israeli plane that had just emptied its arms cargo for his use.
ABNER	Well, it may seem like an extraordinary perspective coming from Ethiopia, but here, in Israel, we're the sole masters of our fate.
ZIV	[...]
ABNER	*(Beat.)* I don't think you're ready for this job.
ZIV	You're wrong, sir.

ABNER	We're under intense scrutiny here. Eager NGO workers, zealous activists, ambitious journalists – monitoring us constantly.
	All waiting for us to slip up.
ZIV	*(Beat.)* I am – ready, sir.
ABNER	People should see when they've been mastered. If they don't, then our duty is to remind them – constantly.
	We can't allow them to think that the status quo can be seized.
	We have a responsibility to reconstitute this world.
	(Beat.) That shit in there is not your family – or your friend. *(Beat.)* He's not even a person.
	(Beat.) See him as a thing – like a table.
	You don't talk to a table, do you?
ZIV	[…]
ABNER	Well, do you?
ZIV	No, sir.
ABNER	Good.
	(Beat.) Because in the end there's no justice in this world.
ZIV	[…]
ABNER	*(Beat.)* And do you know why?
ZIV	No, sir.
ABNER	No.
	(Beat.) Because God forgives us.
	He forgives all our sins.

A LITTLE LONGER

Holding cell.

ABNER	She's fucking hot.
SAEED	[…]

ABNER	I've seen her.
	I know her – intimately.
	I even know when she's on her period.
SAEED	Don't talk about my wife.
ABNER	Her lips, her breasts – and those curves. God, those curves.
	(Beat.) There's no shame in it.
	I'd be on that every night.
SAEED	I told you –
ABNER	*(To ZIV.)* Did you hear that?
ZIV	Sir.
ABNER	*(Beat.)* You remember what I told you?
ZIV	Yes, sir.
ABNER	*(To SAEED.)* You're nothing in here.
	I can talk about anything or anyone I like.
	(Beat.) Do you understand?
	(Beat.) Huh?
SAEED	[…]
ABNER	*(Beat.)* Give me your ring.
SAEED	What?
ABNER	You need to forget all about her.
	Her image will only serve your madness in here – food for dark thoughts.
	She's poison now – let her go.
SAEED	[…]
ABNER	I said give me your ring.

Pause.

SAEED slowly removes his ring and lays it carefully on the floor.

ABNER picks it up.

ABNER	*(Looking at ZIV and pointing towards SAEED.)* What is that?
ZIV	[…]

ABNER	What is it?
ZIV	*(Beat.)* A table.
ABNER	I can't hear you.
ZIV	A table, sir.
ABNER	Good.
ZIV	[...]
ABNER	*(Beat.)* So – go on.
	Show me.
ZIV	[...]
ABNER	[...]
ZIV	*(Beat.)* On your knees.
SAEED	[...]
ZIV	On your fucking knees.

SAEED lowers himself onto his knees.

ZIV	On all fours.
SAEED	[...]
ZIV	Come on.
	Don't make this –
	(Beat.) Get on all fours.

SAEED gets on all fours.

Long pause.

ABNER	Good.
	(Beat.) A table.
ZIV	[...]

ABNER exits.

Long pause.

ZIV	*(Beat.)* I'm sorry.
SAEED	[...]

Pause.

ZIV	I said, I'm sorry.
SAEED	[...]

ZIV	Hey.
	Answer me.
	I told you, I'm sorry.
SAEED	[...]

LOVERS ROCK 1

Prison visiting area.

SAEED and HANEEN are sat across from one another – separated by a thick glass screen.

HANEEN is wearing a hijab.

Long pause.

DOCTOR'S ORDERS

Medical room.

SAEED is sat on a medical examination table – he is evidently in pain.

SARA enters.

SARA	Take it off.
SAEED	[...]
SARA	Take your top off.
SAEED	[...]
SARA	Well, go on.

    SAEED hesitantly removes his top.

SAEED	Are you a doctor?
SARA	Yes.
SAEED	Good.
	(Pointing just above his ribs.) I've got this pain – here.
SARA	We'll get to that. But we need to do a full examination first.
SAEED	Right.

SARA   *(Beat.)* Hey. *(Taking SAEED's hand.)* You're
                going to be fine.

SAEED   […]

SARA   So let's start.

SARA checks SAEED's head.

SAEED winces slightly.

SARA   It's alright.

SARA takes out a penlight.

SARA   *(Checking SAEED's eyes.)* Okay.
                Now, look up.
                Good.

Pause.

SARA   That's great.

Pause.

SARA   *(Showing her index finger.)* Follow my finger.
                Pause.

SARA   Good.
                Pause.

SARA   Good.

SARA takes out an otoscope.

SARA   *(Checking SAEED's ears.)* Now your ears.
                Pause.

SARA   That's good.
                Pause.

SARA   The other.
                Pause.

SARA   Good. Open your mouth, please.

SAEED struggles to open his mouth wide.

SARA   Wider – come on.
                Pause.

SARA	Wider, I said.
SAEED	I can't.
SARA	Does it hurt?
SAEED	Yes.
SARA	Okay.
	(Beat.) Just turn around.

SAEED turns around.

SARA percuses SAEED's back.

SARA takes out a stethoscope.

SARA	*(Placing the stethoscope on SAEED's back.)* Breathe.

Pause.

SARA	Good.
	Again.

Pause.

SARA	Again.

Pause.

SARA	Lie down.
SAEED	But my ribs – I think I've fractured /
SARA	/ Just lie down.

SAEED lies down gingerly – he winces.

SARA	*(Placing the stethoscope on SAEED's chest.)* Breathe.

SAEED struggles inhaling.

SARA checks SAEED's abdomens.

Pause.

SARA	Okay. Sit up.

SAEED sits up.

SARA	The good news is that you're fine.
SAEED	What do you mean?

	(Beat.) Look at me.
SARA	I've just given you a full physical and you're in good shape.
SAEED	My ribs. I can't even – Look at all the bruises – What do you mean I'm fine? Look at my body.
SARA	[…]
SAEED	Look at it.
SARA	Calm down, Saeed.
SAEED	No. Look.
SARA	[…]

Pause.

SARA	Do you have a history of heart trouble in your family?
SAEED	No. Why?
SARA	Well, you've got an irregular heartbeat.
SAEED	No, I don't.
SARA	Now, it could be nothing, but I'd like to keep an eye on it for now. *(Taking out a bottle of pills.)* I want you to take these.
SAEED	What are they?
SARA	*(Placing the bottle on the table.)* Take two a day /
SAEED	/ I said, what are they?
SARA	One at breakfast and another before you sleep.
SAEED	[…]
SARA	*(Taking SAEED's hand.)* It's just a precaution. I'm sure it's nothing.
SAEED	[…]

SARA   You'll be fine.

SARA exits.

SAEED remains transfixed.

THE BIRDWATCHER 1

Two identical adjoining holding cells.

TAREK is lying comfortably on a solid clean mattress reading an Arabic newspaper. While SAEED lies on the filthy floor of the adjoining cell.

SAEED's pained moans.

Long pause.

SAEED's pained moans.

Long pause.

TAREK puts down the newspaper and leans in close to the wall separating the two cells.

Pause.

SAEED   I can't feel my –

    Pause.

SAEED   My – it's numb.

TAREK   Hey.

    Pause.

TAREK   Hey.

              Stay with me now.

    Pause.

TAREK   Hey.

SAEED   Who's there?

              (Beat.) You haven't had enough – you still want /

TAREK   / Hey, hey.

              (Beat.) You want another beating?

              Keep it down.

              (Beat.) The walls here have ears.

SAEED   […]

Pause.

SAEED   I can't feel my –
               I can't feel –

SAEED breaks down.

TAREK   Hey.
               Hey.
               Keep it together.

SAEED   […]

TAREK   It's okay. Trust me – it gets easier.
               (Beat.) Did they give you any medication?

SAEED   *(Beat.)* Some pills.

TAREK   You should take them – they'll help with the
               pain.

SAEED   […]

SAEED takes out the bottle of pills and stares at it.

TAREK   *(Beat.)* Go on – trust me.

SAEED   […]

SAEED puts down the bottle.

SAEED   *(Beat.)* What's the secret?

TAREK   You've got to learn when to throw your
               punches – when they least expect it.
               There's no use flailing in the dark.

SAEED   […]

TAREK   This is where battles are raged – and wars
               won.
               (Beat.) You understand?

SAEED   […]

Pause.

TAREK 5.97219×10^{24} Kg.

SAEED   […]

TAREK 5.97219×10^{24} Kg.

SAEED	What?
TAREK	The weight of the Earth.

SAEED lets out a brief, pained laugh.

TAREK	*(Beat.)* What's your name, friend?
SAEED	159730.
TAREK	No. Your name?
SAEED	[…]

Pause.

SAEED	Saeed Shaka.
TAREK	Good.
	Always remember who you are.
	You're not just rocks and fists.
SAEED	[…]
TAREK	This fight – this fight is of the spirit – not the flesh.
	(Beat.) You hear me?
SAEED	*(Picking up the bottle and looking at it.)* Yes.
TAREK	Good.

SAEED finally opens it and hesitantly swallows two pills.

TAREK	*(Beat.)* And the secret –
	(Beat.) The secret's laughter.
SAEED	[…]
TAREK	You smiling?

SAEED lets out a brief laugh.

TAREK	You must smile – always.
	Don't listen to those people who tell you we don't know how to smile.
	Mask everything with smiles for those fools.
	(Beat.) Smile at the world, Saeed.
	We own nothing except ourselves – these walls leave us nothing else.

SAEED smiles.

TAREK	Saeed.
SAEED	Yes.
TAREK	Are you a God-fearing man?
SAEED	I am.
TAREK	There's no need.
SAEED	[…]
TAREK	Muhammad, peace be upon Him, arrived at the mountaintop and fell asleep. And the Angel Gabriel appeared. *(Beat.)* You know what he told him?

Pause.

| TAREK | He said, "recite, recite, Muhammad. Recite for God who created you. He created mankind from nothing. Recite what he taught you with his writings." |

Pause.

| TAREK | Miraculous. *(Beat.)* Miraculous, my brother. Muhammad is the messenger of God. |

Long pause.

SAEED	You never told me your name?
TAREK	[…]
SAEED	You still there?
TAREK	[…]
SAEED	[…]

LOVERS ROCK 2

Prison visiting area.

SAEED and HANEEN are sat across from one another – separated by a thick glass screen. They are both holding receivers.

| SAEED | How did you manage to get time off? |
| HANEEN | Linda's covering for me – anyway, they've got their mocks this week. |

SAEED	But the promotion? Sara will use anything to /
HANEEN	/ Forget about Sara. She'll understand. And if she doesn't – well – *(Beat.)* I wanted to come – to see you.
SAEED	*(Beat.)* Why hasn't he visited yet?
HANEEN	He tried, Saeed.
SAEED	It's been – *(Beat.)* I don't even know how long it's been – And he still hasn't been to see me. I'm his eldest son.
HANEEN	You know it's not easy for him.
SAEED	He should still – It's not right.
HANEEN	He loves you – you know that.
SAEED	[…]
HANEEN	He's doing everything he can. He's fighting to get you a better lawyer.
SAEED	Why? What's wrong with Bakri?
HANEEN	Nothing. But they're running circles around him – mistranslating documents, sending him to the wrong courts. Bakri's a good friend. He's helped as much as he can – but you need someone who can represent you properly, Saeed.
SAEED	Have they brought any charges yet?
HANEEN	No, they're still refusing to share any evidence. The prosecutor's saying that the material's classified and revealing it could harm national security.
SAEED	But how can we respond without it?
HANEEN	We just have to wait to hear back from the court.

SAEED	*(Beat.)* Who's taking care of the shop?
HANEEN	[…]
SAEED	What is it?
HANEEN	It's not important – not now.
SAEED	Haneen.
HANEEN	They turned it over last week.
SAEED	Turned it over? *(Beat.)* Who did?
HANEEN	Said it was a safe heaven – a potential security threat. *(Beat.)* I don't know.
SAEED	But that's nonsense. They can't believe that – no one would.
HANEEN	I told you, it's not important.
YAEL	*(Offstage.)* Time.
SAEED	[…]
HANEEN	*(Beat.)* I should –
SAEED	Yeah.
HANEEN	I'll be back – as soon as I can. We're going to sort this out.
SAEED	[…]
HANEEN	Hey. It's going to be okay – you hear me. Everything's going to be fine, Saeed.
SAEED	*(Beat.)* I don't want to be by myself anymore.
HANEEN	[…]
SAEED	Don't leave me alone – like this.
HANEEN	I'm here, Saeed – I'm always here.
SAEED	Stay with me a little longer.
HANEEN	[…]
SAEED	Please.
HANEEN	[…]
SAEED	Thank you.
YAEL	*(Offstage.)* Time.
SAEED	Just sit in silence with me.

HANEEN	Okay.

Pause.

SAEED smiles.

Pause.

SAEED	Isn't that beautiful?

TIME

ABNER	Under investigation – secret evidence.
YAEL / ZIV	Administrative detention.

Pause.

SAEED	Forty days.

ASK ME (AGAIN)

Interrogation room.

SAAED is restrained and blindfolded – facing YAEL and ZIV.

ABNER is stood in the corner.

YAEL	Do midgets have night vision?
SAAED	I don't know.
ZIV	Do porcupines masturbate?
SAEED	I don't know.
YAEL	How many rings make up an arm on a Michelin Man?
SAEED	I don't know.
ZIV	What salad dressing does the 'special sauce' on a Big Mac most closely resemble?
SAEED	I don't know.
YAEL	What is the Armenian raw meat dish similar to steak tartare?
SAEED	[…]
ZIV	How do you make chickens quack?

SAEED	[…]
YAEL	Why did the chicken cross the road?
SAEED	[…]
ZIV	Chicken? Egg? Which came first?
SAEED	[…]
YAEL	Where is he?
ZIV	Where is he?
YAEL	Where is he?
ZIV	Where is he?
YAEL	Where is he?
ZIV	Where is he?
YAEL	Where is he?
ZIV	Where is he?

GOOGLE IT

Interrogation room.

ABNER and SAEED are sat at a table.

ZIV is stood in the corner.

ABNER	It's not the same – the world as it is. It's all on its ass these days.
	(Beat.) But you know it doesn't have to be this way – like this.
SAEED	[…]
ABNER	This doesn't have to be your fate, Saeed. It's not too late.
	You could end this right now – all of it.
	All you have to do is tell us where your brother is.
SAEED	[…]
ABNER	*(Beat.)* Come on, Saeed. I'm trying to help you out here.
	We know you were with him.

SAEED	I don't know what you're talking about.
ABNER	He's got blood on his hands – your brother. Our people's blood.
	You shouldn't have to pay the price for his actions.
	(Beat.) He won't get away with it. You know that. The mouse has to come out of his hole eventually. So you might as well save everyone the trouble – and all that pain you're sure to incur.
SAEED	You're lying.
ABNER	Think about your family, Saeed.
SAEED	Don't – *(Beat.)* don't try and –
Pause.	
SAEED	I have nothing to say.
ABNER	With everything you've got left to lose – it's almost tragic.
	Think of how your wife's feeling right now.
	(Beat.) Can you imagine?
SAEED	[…]
ABNER	Just give me a reason to stop, Saeed – and I will.
SAEED	[…]
ABNER	*(Beat.)* Okay.
	As you wish.
	(To ZIV.) Wait outside.
ZIV	But sir –
ABNER	*(To ZIV.)* Now.
ZIV	*(Beat.)* Yes, sir.
ZIV exits.	
Pause.	

ABNER   It was planned impeccably – the detail, the
                imagination, the sheer audacity of it all.
                (Beat.) I'll give him that.
                Soldiers said they could hear the mower
                engines roar above their station.
                (Beat.) But six men were murdered that night
                – two of them I knew. Close friends, they
                were.
                You should have seen the headlines the next
                morning – they called it the Night of the
                Gliders. It was a fucking mess. Ehud Barak
                vowed that the PFLP would pay the ultimate
                price – and eventually they did.

ABNER becomes more physically intimidating.

                But your people's smugness.
                I was still a boy at the time – stationed
                in Gaza. You used to taunt us every day
                with cries of 'six to one' – seeing that shit
                graffitied everywhere.
                (Beat.) I never met him myself – but we
                all knew of him. His aura. And how he
                managed to mastermind the whole attack
                from the West Bank.
                I should take you to Kiryat Shmona – show
                you the monument there. Let you see it for
                yourself.
                (Beat.) It's in your people's makeup.
                It must just run through your blood – in your
                family's DNA.

SAEED   You don't understand a thing.

ABNER   Prove me wrong then. Tell me where your
                brother is.

SAEED   [...]

ABNER becomes increasingly forceful.

ABNER   I know your people have nothing but
                vengeance ingrained in their hearts.

	It's a disease – a cancer.
SAEED	*(Beat.)* I don't know where he is.
ABNER	[…]
SAEED	I want to see my lawyer.
	I have a right to speak to my lawyer.
ABNER	[…]

Pause.

| ABNER | Guard. |

Pause.

| ABNER | Guard. |

ZIV enters.

| ABNER | He's wasting my time. |
| | *(Beat.)* Get him out of here. |

ABNER takes out a packet of cigarettes – and lights one.

| ZIV | Yes, sir. |

ZIV restrains SAEED and removes him from the room.

THE BIRDWATCHER 2

Two identical adjoining holding cells.

TAREK is lying on a mattress listening to music on a Walkman.

Pause.

YAEL brings SAEED into the adjoining cell.

YAEL unshackles SAEED.

YAEL exits.

ABNER enters TAREK's cell.

ABNER throws a file into TAREK's lap.

ABNER	Off.
TAREK	[…]
ABNER	Tarek – take them off.
TAREK	*(Removing his headphones.)* What?

ABNER sits on a stool in the corner.

ABNER points to the adjoining cell.

TAREK   […]

TAREK moves closer to the wall.

ABNER takes out a tape recorder.

TAREK begins flicking through the file.

Pause.

TAREK   Hey.

Pause.

TAREK   Hey, Saeed.

Pause.

TAREK   Saeed. You there?

Pause.

TAREK   […]

ABNER   *(Urging him on.)* […]

Pause.

TAREK   Saeed. It's okay – it's me.

Pause.

SAEED   *(Beat.)* You never told me your name?

Pause.

TAREK   Ghassan.
               Ghassan Hadawi.

SAEED   Ghassan.

TAREK   Yes.

SAEED   I don't know if I can do this.

TAREK   […]

SAEED   What if the world forgets me – while I'm
               here?
               What if I see nothing new again in my life?

TAREK   All our movement in this world – it's just
               noise, Saeed.

SAEED	But what if it all passes me by? *(Beat.)* Standing here for the rest of my life – still – just in one spot.
TAREK	I've remained still now for longer than I can remember.
	I can stay like this for the rest of my life – assured that there's nowhere else.
	I'm not going to find anything more.
	And neither will you, Saeed.
SAEED	[…]
TAREK	Be still, Saeed. Be still. It's the door to the biggest infinity possible.
SAEED	[…]
TAREK	*(Beat.)* So what was the question?
SAEED	What?
TAREK	The one they kept asking you.
SAEED	*(Beat.)* Where is he?
TAREK	Who are they talking about?
SAEED	My brother, I think.
TAREK	Your brother.
SAEED	Talal's a troublemaker – a firebrand. He hasn't learnt how to pick his battles yet.
	He'll soon learn though.
TAREK	[…]
ABNER	[…]
TAREK	*(Beat.)* So what's his – thing?
SAEED	What do you mean?
TAREK	Arms, religion, money laundering, drugs –
SAEED	I don't know.
TAREK	Right.
ABNER	[…]
TAREK	You sound like you're close – you and Talal.
SAEED	He's a good kid – finding his way still.

TAREK	They all are.

Pause.

SAEED	*(Beat.)* I saw him last week.
TAREK	[…]
SAEED	He needed some money.
TAREK	Right.
SAEED	He's the youngest, you know – and he needed help.
	It's my responsibility.
TAREK	Of course.

ABNER switches off the tape recorder.

TAREK	This was in the bookshop?
SAEED	Sorry?
TAREK	You met him in your shop?
SAEED	*(Beat.)* What did you say?
TAREK	[…]
SAEED	How do you know about my bookshop?
	I never –
	(Beat.) Hey –

YAEL and ZIV rush into SAEED's cell.

SAEED	*(Beat.)* Hey. *(Beat.)* Hey. *(Beat.)* Answer me.
	(Beat.) Hey.

YAEL and ZIV restrain SAEED.

Pause.

TAREK throws the file on the floor beside ABNER and exits.

ABNER remains seated – lighting a cigarette.

TIME

ABNER	For activities that threaten regional security.
YAEL / ZIV	Sentence deferred.

Pause.

SAEED   Six months.

PICK YOUR TEAM

Israeli Prison.

Room.

ABNER   Fatah, Hamas or Islamic Jihad?

SAEED   I don't understand.

ABNER   Your affiliation – allegiance.

SAEED   I don't know. I don't have one.

ABNER   Everyone has one – a side.
         Who are you with?

SAEED   […]

ABNER   You're wasting my time.
         (Beat.) Do you want to survive in here?

SAEED   Yes.

ABNER   Then pick one – whichever. *(Beat.)* It's not
         like it matters.

SAEED   […]

ABNER   *(Beat.)* Okay. Why don't we just throw you
         into solitary? Until you make up your mind?

SAEED   No.

ABNER   Well then?

SAEED   […]

 Pause.

ABNER   *(To ZIV.) (Beat.)* Go on.

ZIV   Off.

SAEED   […]

ZIV   Take your clothes off.

 Pause.

SAEED slowly disrobes.

Pause.

SAEED is left in his underwear.

ZIV   Everything.

SAEED   […]

YAEL   Did you hear him?

Pause.

SAEED takes off his underwear.

ZIV   Hands up.

SAEED raises his hands.

ZIV   Higher.

SAEED raises his hands higher.

ABNER   Are you religious?

SAEED   What?

ABNER   Your religion – sect?

SAEED   […]

ZIV   Palms out.

SAEED shows his palms.

ABNER   Do you go to prayers?

SAEED   Yes – not all the time. Sometimes.

ABNER   *(Beat.)* Just give me straight answers.

ZIV   Shake your hair.

SAEED shakes his hair out.

ZIV   Mouth open.

SAEED opens his mouth.

ABNER   Any dietary requirements?

SAEED   No. Nothing unusual.

ZIV   Tongue out.

SAEED sticks his tongue out.

             Turn around.

SAEED turns around.

> Bottom of your feet.

SAEED lifts his foot.

> The other.

SAEED lifts his other foot.

> Bend over.

SAEED bends over.

> Cough.

SAEED coughs.

ABNER   Give him a uniform and pair of shoes.

ZIV collects a new uniform and pair of shoes, and hands them over to SAEED.

YAEL   We should take those pills off him.

ABNER   No.

YAEL   But it /

ABNER   / I said not now – it's too early.

YAEL   […]

ABNER   So? *(Beat.)* You chosen yet?

SAEED   No.

ABNER   *(Beat.)* Fine.

       (To YAEL.) Put him in solitary.

ISOLATION 1

Solitary confinement.
A blinding, flickering light bulb.
A ladder is painted on the cell wall – all the way up to the top.
YAEL enters with SAEED.
Pause.

YAEL   You see that?

SAEED   […]

YAEL   That's how the last one got out.

SAEED   […]

YAEL   *(Beat.)* You should try your luck – you never know.

SAEED   […]

YAEL   *(Beat.)* Give me your pills.

SAEED   No.

YAEL   Give them to me.

SAEED   […]

YAEL   Now, I said.

SAEED takes out the bottle of pills and hands them over to YAEL.

SAEED   Please.

YAEL   You want them?

SAEED   Yes.

YAEL   Then get on your knees.

SAEED   […]

YAEL   Don't you want them?

SAEED lowers himself onto his knees.

YAEL opens the bottle and takes out two pills – placing them in the palm of her hand. She then extends her hand towards SAEED.

YAEL   Take.

SAEED   […]

YAEL   Go on – we don't want your heart to explode now, do we?

SAEED slowly extends his hand to take the pills.

YAEL   No. *(Beat.)* With your mouth.

SAEED   […]

Pause.

SAEED takes the pills in his mouth and swallows them.

YAEL throws the bottle to the ground.

YAEL exits.

Long pause.

SAEED looks at the painted wall – touching it hesitantly – feeling his way around it.

Pause.

SAEED sits in the corner.

Long pause.

MEALTIME

Solitary confinement.

A blinding, flickering light bulb.

SAEED is sat in the corner.

Pause.

ZIV	*(Sliding a meal tray into the cell.)* Morning.
	Dinner.
	(Beat.) Eat up.
ABNER	Have you chosen?
SAEED	*(Ignoring the meal tray.)* […]

Long pause.

YAEL	*(Sliding a meal tray into the cell.)* Evening.
	Lunch.
	Chicken – yum.
	(Beat.) Eat up.
ABNER	Have you chosen?
SAEED	*(Ignoring the meal tray.)* […]

Long pause.

ZIV	*(Sliding a meal tray into the cell.)* Afternoon.
	Breakfast.
	(Beat.) Eat up.
ABNER	Have you chosen?
SAEED	*(Ignoring the meal tray.)* […]

ISOLATION 2

Solitary confinement.

A blinding, flickering light bulb.

SAEED is sat in the corner.

Pause.

SAEED takes out the bottle of pills. He's quicker this time – opening it and swallowing two pills.

Pause.

YAEL enters carrying a paintbrush and pot of paint.

Pause.

YAEL begins to paint a bicycle on the cell wall.

Pause.

Once YAEL finishes painting the bicycle, she collects the paintbrush and pot.

Pause.

YAEL	I used to love riding my bicycle as a little girl. *(Beat.)* Go on. Get on it – give it a spin.
SAEED	[…]
YAEL	No?
SAEED	[…]
YAEL	You could do with the exercise, you know.
SAEED	[…]
YAEL	Go on. It'll be fun.
SAEED	[…]

YAEL exits.

Long pause.

SAEED gets up and looks at the painted bicycle – touching it hesitantly – feeling his way around it.

Pause.

SAEED tries to get on the painted bicycle and ride it.

Pause.

SAEED laughs and screams with sheer delight as he pretends to ride the painted bicycle around the cell.

Pause.

SAEED   The wind. The wind in my face. *(Beat.)* Yes. I
               can feel it.
               The wind in my face.
               (Beat.) But the –

Pause.

SAEED   But the leaves.
               There's – there's blood on the leaves.
               There's blood on the leaves.
               Hey. *(Beat.)* Hey.
               There's blood on the leaves.
               Hey. *(Beat.)* Hey.

MEALTIME

Solitary confinement.
A blinding, flickering light bulb.
SAEED is sat in the corner.
Pause.

ZIV   *(Sliding a meal tray into the cell.)* Morning.
               Dinner.
               (Beat.) Eat up.
ABNER   Have you chosen?
SAEED   *(Ignoring the meal tray.)* […]

   Long pause.

YAEL   *(Sliding a meal tray into the cell.)* Evening.
               Lunch.
               Chicken – yum.
               (Beat.) Eat up.
ABNER   Have you chosen?

SAEED	*(Ignoring the meal tray.)* […]

Long pause.

ZIV	*(Sliding a meal tray into the cell.)* Afternoon.
	Breakfast.
	(Beat.) Eat up.
ABNER	Have you chosen?
SAEED	*(Ignoring the meal tray.)* Yes.

Pause.

SAEED	Enough. Please.
	(Beat.) I've had enough.
	I can't –

ISOLATION 3

Solitary confinement.
A blinding, flickering light bulb.
SAEED is sat in the corner.

Pause.

ABNER enters.

ABNER	Get up.
SAEED	[…]
ABNER	Come on – on your feet.

SAEED struggles to pick himself up.

Long pause.

ABNER	So you picked yet?
SAEED	[…]
ABNER	There's no rush – we can keep you /
SAEED	*(Shouting.)* / No.
ABNER	[…]
SAEED	*(Beat.)* No.
	I've chosen.

ABNER   Well then? *(Beat.)* Who will it be?

   Pause.

SAEED   Fatah.

A NEW HOME

Cell.

Two bunk beds. One of the beds is perfectly made up. A video player and old, beat-up television are stacked in one corner.

MUHIB is sat listening to the news on the radio.

SHADI is sat reading a comic book.

Pause.

YAEL enters with SAEED.

MUHIB   [...]

YAEL   Over there.

               (Beat.) Move.

   YAEL unshackles SAEED.

MUHIB   Who's this?

YAEL   Newbie.

MUHIB   [...]

   MUHIB looks at SAEED.

YAEL   Play nice now.

MUHIB   *(To YAEL.)* Well?

YAEL   What?

MUHIB   You got it?

YAEL   Yeah.

MUHIB   So?

YAEL   Not on me though.

MUHIB   Where is it?

YAEL   Don't worry – I've got it.

MUHIB   I need it.

YAEL   [...]

MUHIB   It's Friday. *(Beat.)* We had a deal – an
               expensive deal at that.

YAEL   You'll get it.

MUHIB   […]

YAEL   *(Beat.)* What? Now?

MUHIB   If you want your money, yeah.

YAEL   Fuck Muhib – you're going to put me in the
               shit one of these days.

MUHIB   You don't like it, stop. I'll find someone else
               – easy.

YAEL   […]

MUHIB   *(Beat.)* Go sort it out then.

YAEL exits.

MUHIB goes back to his radio.

Pause.

SAEED   […]

Pause.

SAEED   […]

Pause.

MUHIB   You just going to stand there – like that?
               (Beat.) Sit down.

SAEED sits down on the opposite bunk.

SHADI   Not there – that's Akram's.
               (Beat.) The other one.

SAEED sits on the other bed.

Pause.

MUHIB   What's your name son?

SAEED   Saeed

MUHIB   Saeed what?

SAEED   Saeed Shaka.

MUHIB   Shaka – from Nablus, right?

SAEED	Yes.
MUHIB	So who's Khalil Shaka to you then?
SAEED	He's my father.
MUHIB	The property developer.
SAEED	You know him?
MUHIB	No.
SAEED	[...]
MUHIB	*(Beat.)* And Talal?
SAEED	My brother.
MUHIB	The fighter.
	He's a good man – your brother.
SAEED	[...]
MUHIB	*(Beat.)* And you? *(Beat.)* What's your story?
SAEED	Nothing.
MUHIB	Come on – everyone's got a story.
SAEED	I have a bookshop.
MUHIB	In Nablus?
SAEED	Souq Al-Thahab Street.
MUHIB	A property developer, a fighter and a bookshop owner – quite the family yours.
	And of those three, it's the bookshop owner who finds himself stuck in here.
	That's Israel for you.
SAEED	[...]

YAEL enters.

YAEL	*(Throwing a mobile phone on the bed.)* Here.

MUHIB picks up the mobile and checks it thoroughly.

YAEL	Alright?
MUHIB	[...]

YAEL prepares to leave.

MUHIB	Wait.
YAEL	What?

MUHIB	What? *(Beat.)* Where's the charger?
YAEL	The charger's extra.
MUHIB	*(Laughing.)* Come on Yael – stop fucking about.
	(Beat.) Go get me the charger.
YAEL	You need to remember your place in here.
MUHIB	Okay – just get it.
YAEL	You want the charger – it'll cost you.
MUHIB	Don't mess me /
YAEL	/ That's the deal, Muhib.
	And I expect my money from Taher – all of it – and on time.
	(Beat.) Are we clear?
MUHIB	[…]
YAEL	*(Beat.)* Good.

YAEL exits.

SHADI	Fucking cunts.
MUHIB	The lot of them.

LOVERS ROCK 3

Prison visiting area.
SAEED is sat waiting.
Pause.
SAEED tidies himself up.
Pause.

SAEED	*(Fixing his hair.)* How do I look?

Pause.

SAEED	*(Looking in the glass screen.)* Yeah. I look good.

Pause.

SAEED	*(Beat.)* You look – you look so lovely.
	I wish I could – just touch you.

Pause.

SAEED	Do you remember the first time we met?
	(Laughing.) He wasn't too happy.
	He knew – your father.
	(Beat.) Fathers always know.

Pause.

SAEED	I love you. You know that.

HANEEN enters.

SAEED	[...]

SAEED *and* HANEEN *sit across from one another – separated by a thick glass screen.*

HANEEN picks up the receiver.

Pause.

SAEED picks up the receiver.

Pause.

HANEEN	How are you?
SAEED	[...]
HANEEN	Saeed.
SAEED	[...]
HANEEN	Saeed.
	Talk to me.
SAEED	[...]
HANEEN	Saeed, you need to talk.

Pause.

SAEED	*(Beat.)* You want to know?
HANEEN	Yes. Of course I do.
	I'm worried about you.
SAEED	Do you? *(Beat.)* Really?
HANEEN	I deserve to know, Saeed.
	(Beat.) Why are you being –
SAEED	/ I shake.

(Beat.) My head rings.

Shit.

Pause.

SAEED   I sweat.

(Beat.) I sweat.

SAEED   I can't feel –

Pause.

SAEED   My heart. *(Beat.)* It pounds.

SAEED takes out the bottle and quickly swallows two pills.

HANNEN   What are those?

SAEED   Sometimes my heart just –

HANEEN   Saeed.

SAEED   You still want to know.

HANEEN   Saeed. Who gave them to you?

SAEED   I can't sleep.

HANEEN   Look at me.

SAEED   I can't eat.

Pause.

SAEED   I can't shit.

Pause.

SAEED   I feel –

I feel like –

HANEEN   Saeed. Please.

SAEED   I feel like –

HANEEN   Saeed.

Saeed, listen to me.

SAEED   I don't know how – I feel.

(Beat.) And still my father won't come.

HANEEN   […]

SAEED   Why isn't he here? Still – after all this time.

HANEEN   […]

SAEED	Tell me.
HANEEN	He's trying – he is, I promise you.
	But things are difficult.
SAEED	It's the development, isn't it?
	He's embarrassed – worried about how it might look.
HANEEN	[…]
SAEED	*(Beat.)* Of course he is.
HANEEN	*(Beat.)* This isn't your father's fault, you know.
SAEED	[…]
HANEEN	He didn't get you arrested.
SAEED	What does that mean?
HANEEN	You promised me, Saaed.
SAEED	[…]
HANEEN	You said.
SAEED	Said what?
HANEEN	You promised me that your brother wouldn't ruin things for us.
SAEED	This has nothing to do with Talal.
HANEEN	No.
SAEED	I didn't do anything, Haneen.
	(Beat.) What could I be involved in?
HANEEN	I don't know.
	I don't know what to think anymore.
SAEED	[…]
HANEEN	*(Beat.)* They asked me about him – Talal.
SAEED	So now you're talking to them?
	What did you tell them?
HANEEN	Nothing.
SAEED	There's something you're not telling me.
	What did they ask?

HANEEN	About your connection to him.
SAEED	He's my brother. What do they expect?
HANEEN	*(Beat.)* Did you see him? *(Beat.)* Before all this.
SAEED	What do you want from me – to disown him like my father? I'm his older brother. I won't just leave him – watch him ruin his life.
HANEEN	Did you, Saeed?
SAEED	[…]
HANEEN	Don't lie to me.
SAEED	*(Beat.)* No. I didn't.
HANEEN	*(Beat.)* God, I hope you're telling me the truth.
SAEED	[…]

Pause.

SAEED	*(Beat.)* Do you remember the first time we met?
HANEEN	Why?
SAEED	Do you?
HANEEN	Of course.
SAEED	*(Beat.)* Really?
HANEEN	[…]
SAEED	*(Beat.)* Because I don't.

SHOOTING THE BREEZE

Cell.

SAEED is reading one of SHADI's comic books.

MUHIB is cutting his toenails.

SHADI is fiddling with the television and video player.

SHADI	Piece of shit.

We need a new TV.

SAEED *and* MUHIB	[...]
SHADI	Can't you both just give me a few minutes – to myself?
SAEED *and* MUHIB	[...]
SHADI	Come on guys. *(Waving a VHS tape.)* The sequel's just arrived – and I'm fucking horny.
SAEED *and* MUHIB	[...]
SHADI	*(Beat.)* You know how much it cost me?
SHADI	This one's set in a palace – I love porn set in palaces. The girls are prettier, better dressed – and cleaner, much cleaner. They don't look like the usual sluts. *(Beat.)* It makes such a difference when you want to come real fast –
SAEED *and* MUHIB	[...]
SHADI	It won't take me long. Honestly. I'll be quick. *(Beat.)* Muhib. *(Beat.)* Saeed. *(Beat.)* For the cause – for my desperate fucking cause.
MUHIB	*(Picking up a newspaper.)* Didn't you already have a wank today? I heard you tugging away in bed this morning.
SHADI	Yeah. *(Beat.)* That was the morning though – it's already late afternoon.
MUHIB	[...]
SHADI	*(Beat.)* You can borrow it when I'm done. I won't tell anyone.

MUHIB	I'm alright.
	(Beat.) Where's my Turkish soaps? I couldn't find them last night.
SHADI	[…]
MUHIB	Where are they?
SHADI	I don't know.
MUHIB	*(Beat.)* You haven't?
SHADI	What?
MUHIB	You have.
SHADI	No.
MUHIB	You've recorded over them again.
SHADI	No – no, I wouldn't.
	Anyway, I don't understand why you watch that shit – *What is Fatmagül's Fault?*
	You need to get into what I'm watching.
MUHIB	[…]
SHADI	There was this one crazy scene – with a chauffeur.
MUHIB	[…]
SHADI	She had the gearshift in her – I mean *in* her.
	He then fucks her from her behind, slaps her big ass a little – all in the front seat of his limousine.
	It's incredible.
MUHIB	You've lost your mind.
SHADI	I think he was still driving too.
SAEED	I don't get this – *(Looking at the comic book.)* Batman.
	Why does he decide to fight crime?
SHADI	After the murder of his parents when he was a child.
SAEED	The rich socialites?
SHADI	Yeah – by this evil small-time criminal.

SAEED   So it's the story of an elite superhero
                 preserving the idea that there's good
                 rich people who can save our cities from
                 their worst excesses.

SHADI   Uhm. *(Beat.)* Yeah. *(Beat.)* I guess so.

SAEED   Sounds all too familiar.
                 (Beat.) You got anything else?

SHADI   Maybe – check under my bed.

SAEED starts digging under SHADI's mattress.

SAEED   *(Looking at the untouched bed.)* So what's with
                 Akram?

MUHIB   [...]

SHADI   [...]

SAEED   *(Beat.)* What? Is he your imaginary friend or
                 something?

MUHIB   Shut your mouth.

SHADI   Muhib.

SAEED   What did I say?

MUHIB   You're talking shit.

SAEED   Hey. I was just joking.

SHADI   It's alright.

SAEED   Clearly not.

SHADI   Just drop it, Saeed.

SAEED   [...]

Pause.

SAEED carries on digging under SHADI's mattress.

Pause.

MUHIB   *(Holding up a page from the newspaper.)* You
                 seen this?

SAEED   [...]

SHADI   What is it?

MUHIB   The dream of a Palestinian middle class in
                     the West Bank.

                     (Beat.) An interview with council member,
                     Khalil Shaka.

SAEED   […]

MUHIB   What do you make of that, Saaed?

                     (Beat.) Look at that shining city on a hill.

SAEED   I don't know – nothing.

MUHIB   *(Reading.)* […]

                     By building large-scale, affordable housing,
                     they hope to help nurture a fledgling middle
                     class in a society that straddles two economic
                     tiers – rich and poor. Home prices will
                     range from million-dollar mansions – mostly
                     unattainable in an area with a per capita
                     income of $1,554 – to cheap flats. *(Beat.)* 'We
                     saw the impact of real estate,' says Khalil
                     Shaka. 'We saw how real estate can create
                     jobs fast – very fast. We saw how the people
                     who bought, who could not buy before, felt
                     more at ease and more secure by owning
                     their own home – even if it's a cheaper place
                     to begin with. So that's what gave us the
                     idea to create Rawabi in 2007. This is very
                     important for young families who have not
                     managed to save up much money. If you're a
                     couple and making a thousand dollars a
                     month, that's enough for you to start buying
                     a home at –

SAEED   Stop.

SHADI   There's no way I'm making that kind of
                     money.

MUHIB   Your father must be raking it in.

SAEED   Why do you care so much?

MUHIB   Paid for that expensive education of yours
                     with the debts of others.

SAEED	What's your problem?
MUHIB	My problem?
SHADI	Come on, Muhib.
SAEED	What is it you want from me?
MUHIB	I don't know – to see whether or not we can trust you.
SHADI	It's not his fault – he's not responsible for what his father does.
	That whole generation's fucking corrupt – look at all those PA cunts.
SAEED	And you doubt me because /
MUHIB	/ Because you're the son of a traitor.
	Because you don't really know someone until you know what they want.
SAEED	You don't know what you're talking about.
MUHIB	Don't I?
	(Beat.) And why do you think I've been in prison for over twenty years?
	(Beat.) The truth may be a slippery worm, but I know what happened – what was done to me. I'll never forget that.
SAEED	[...]
MUHIB	You have no idea, son.
	Maybe you should ask your father.
SAEED	*(Beat.)* What's my father got to do with it?

MUHIB smiles.

SAEED	Tell me.
MUHIB	*(Beat.)* Be careful what you ask for. You might not like what you find.

TIME

ABNER	For activities that threaten regional security.
YAEL / ZIV	Sentence deferred.

Pause.

SAEED   Six months.

EXERCISE 1

Courtyard.

> *SAEED is jogging steadily in a circle.*
>
> *YAEL is stood still in the centre.*
>
> *Long pause.*
>
> *SAEED begins to pick up the pace.*
>
> *Pause.*

YAEL   Slow down.

> *Pause.*

YAEL   Slow down, I said.
                      Pace yourself – it's not a race.

> *SAEED gradually slows down to a steady pace.*
>
> *Long pause.*

YAEL   We got him – your brother.
                      Targeted prevention.
                      He'd managed to escape arrest a few days earlier, but we found him in the end – hiding in a cave near Kufr Nemeh.

> *SAEED picks it up again.*
>
> *Pause.*

YAEL   Stop running like you're being chased.
                      (Beat.) Remember. You must pace yourself – always.

MAKING HEADLINES

Room.

CLAIRE is sat at a long table. She is busy flicking through her notes.

Pause.

ZIV	*(Offstage.)* Get it now.
SHADI	*(Offstage.)* You think you can shut me up.
	(Beat.) Fuck you. Take off these handcuffs.

CLAIRE stops – staring at the door.

ZIV	*(Offstage.)* You think you're being clever – I won't forget this.
SHADI	*(Offstage.)* Just calm down – calm it.
	(Beat.) Hey. Don't touch me. That fucking – I told you to stop pulling.
	(Beat.) I can walk by myself.

Pause.

SHADI enters. He is wearing a Na'vi costume from the film 'Avatar'.

Pause.

SHADI	*(Rubbing his wrists.)* Sorry about that.
CLAIRE	[…]

Pause.

SHADI	*(Sitting down.)* Tough nut that one. Needs a good –
CLAIRE	*(Beat.)* A good what?
SHADI	*(Beat.)* Hug.

Pause.

CLAIRE	*(Beat.)* Are you just going to –
SHADI	What?
CLAIRE	It's funny. I get it – very clever.
	So –
SHADI	[…]

CLAIRE	*(Beat.)* Okay. I'm just going to –
SHADI	[…]
CLAIRE	*(Beat.)* No – okay.
	So, Shadi Habash, right?
SHADI	[…]
CLAIRE	I'm sorry. Is this some –
SHADI	Joke. *(Beat.)* Maybe – if it gets us in your paper.
	Whatever you need me to be?
CLAIRE	Need you to be?
SHADI	In this case, the sapient humanoid indigenous inhabitant of a fictional moon.
	(Beat.) Or I could just get my cock out and dance around this room naked?
	(Beat.) Curse my religion and piss on a Koran or something?
	(Beat.) Something else?
	You can get your camera crew in and film me doing whatever you want.
	Turn me into an artist. Because those are the only people you care about these days, right – artists.
CLAIRE	[…]
SHADI	*(Removing the wig and mask.)* What I say in here isn't going anywhere – anywhere that matters. You know that.
	It's just going to suffocate and die in that notepad of yours. *(Beat.)* Maybe earn you a pat on the back though, right?
CLAIRE	That's not true – or fair.
SHADI	What's fair?
	Pause.
CLAIRE	*(Beat.)* Why don't we try again – start again – from the beginning?

82

SHADI	[…]
CLAIRE	*(Beat.)* Okay. So /
SHADI	/ Who do you write for again?
CLAIRE	Uhm. I freelance.
SHADI	So no one.
CLAIRE	No. I'm published – *The Guardian*, *The New Statesman*. *(Beat.)* On their blogs.
SHADI	Right.
CLAIRE	*(Beat.)* So you were arrested on terrorism-related charges – aiding and abetting.
SHADI	Sure.
CLAIRE	And when is your hearing?
SHADI	Don't know.
	I'm still waiting – I've been waiting for nearly a year now.
	(Beat.) What's your name again?
CLAIRE	Claire.
SHADI	That's a nice name – simple.
	(Beat.) You married, Claire?
CLAIRE	That's – I don't think that's really /
SHADI	/ Any of my business. *(Beat.)* Right.
CLAIRE	Listen. You can carry on like this – being aggressive – wasting both our time. It makes no difference to me.
	But don't you want people to hear your side of things? *(Beat.)* Hear about what's really going on here?

SHADI smiles.

CLAIRE	I'm not the enemy Shadi.
SHADI	No. You're not.
	But that doesn't make you my friend.
CLAIRE	[…]

Pause.

SHADI	*(Beat.)* You want to hear a joke?
CLAIRE	[…]
SHADI	Well, do you?
	(Beat.) It's funny. Trust me.
CLAIRE	*(Beat.)* Go on then.
SHADI	You're going to love it.

Okay. So, there's this fat old man – I mean fat, fat – real fat – and he's living all alone in Hebron. His wife past away ten years ago and his only son Faisal is in an Israeli prison. The old man wants to plant some potatoes in his garden, but he doesn't have the strength – he's fat, remember – and he's got no one to help him.

(Beat.) You following?

CLAIRE	Yeah.
SHADI	Good.

Okay. So the old man writes to his son – 'I want to plant some potatoes in our garden, but I don't have the strength to work the soil anymore. *(Beat.)* What should I do, son?'

Right, so the son gets the letter, reads it and writes back, 'whatever you do, don't go anywhere near the garden – I hid weapons there!'

Now, when the fat old man reads his son's letter, he's shocked and stays away from the garden.

The next morning, the old man is woken by the sound of Israeli soldiers flooding into his garden. He looks out of his window and watches them dig up the whole garden, searching for weapons. *(Beat.)* But they find nothing.

Mystified, the fat old man writes to his son again – 'the soldiers came and dug up our garden, but they didn't find any weapons. What should I do?'

(Beat.) The son writes back and says; 'now you can plant those potatoes.'

CLAIRE   […]

SHADI   *(Beat.)* You get it?

UNDER THE MATTRESS

Cell.

ABNER, YAEL and ZIV enter.

ABNER   Routine check.

SHADI   Again.

               Come on. You just /

ABNER   / Shut up. *(Beat.)* Move – up against the wall.

SHADI   Fuck's sake.

 MUHIB, SHADI and SAEED slowly move up against the wall.

ABNER   Come on – I don't have all day. Move.
               (Beat.) Move.

 Pause.

ABNER   *(To YAEL and ZIV.)* Go on.

               Leave nothing.

 YAEL and ZIV start turning the cell over.

ABNER   You think this a hotel – some kind of holiday camp?

MUHIB, SHADI
&SAEED   […]

 YAEL and ZIV continue turning the cell over.

ABNER   We're not your housekeepers. *(Beat.)* Your maids.

MUHIB, SHADI
&SAEED   […]

As YAEL and ZIV flip their beds, rip their sheets and gut their mattresses, they find – and toss out with complete disregard – hidden money, cigarettes, VHS tapes, porn magazines, comic books and other personal items.

ABNER   Fucking animals.

      (Beat.) Things are going to change around here.

YAEL removes a mobile phone.

YAEL   Sir.

ABNER   *(Taking the phone.)* […]

Pause.

ABNER   Whose is this?

MUHIB, SHADI
&SAEED   […]

ABNER   You know the rules – you've all been here long enough. No phones.

MUHIB, SHADI
&SAEED   […]

ABNER   Don't waste my time – I'm only going to ask you once.

MUHIB, SHADI
&SAEED   […]

YAEL   It was under Muhib's mattress, sir.

ABNER   […]

MUHIB   […]

ABNER   *(To MUHIB.)* Well?

MUHIB   It's not mine.

ABNER   Whose is it then?

MUHIB   I don't know.

ABNER   You don't know.

      (Beat.) Well, that's a problem.

Pause.

SAEED   It's mine.

MUHIB	[...]
ABNER	*(Beat.)* Yours?
SAEED	Yes.
ABNER	You sure, Saeed?
	You don't want to think again?
SAEED	No – it's mine.
ABNER	So you're playing hero now?
SAEED	I'm not.
ABNER	I'm going to give you one last chance.
SAEED	[...]

Pause.

ABNER	Okay then. As you wish.
	You know what this means.
	(Beat.) Take him out.

YAEL and ZIV shackle SAEED and drag him out of the cell.

Pause.

ABNER	*(Beat.)* Clear up this mess.

ABNER exits.

HEADLINE NEWS

Room.

ABNER	*(Holding the mobile.)* You see. They mock us – try and turn the law into a simple inconvenience.
CLAIRE	It's a phone.
ABNER	A vicious circle is what it is.
	The rule of law is about more than simply the enforcement of the defined norms of a given legal system. It's about confidence and reliance – the confidence and reliance of every individual that justice will be done.

CLAIRE	But the law, your law, which is in the hands of one people, is being systematically applied on another.
	(Beat.) Is that just?
ABNER	Order and justice don't always go hand in hand – especially not in this part of the world.
	I come from the free world. A world where, if I want to ask someone a question, I ask. And if he doesn't want to answer, he doesn't have to. I can't twist his arm and force him. And then you arrive here, a gray world, in which my purpose is to protect people from the possibility that some day, these people, they might come and kill you.
	You have to remember that, at the end of the day, they want to throw us out of this land.
	But we aren't here because of some mystical belief in ushering in the Messiah and a Jewish kingdom.
	This country's going nowhere – we're going nowhere.
CLAIRE	I understand. But don't you think some of your methods could be having an undesired effect? Instigating another generation who have nothing to lose?
ABNER	Absolutely not. I don't see any evidence to support such a claim.
	Israel is not America – or Britain. We are in a permanent state of war here.
	(Beat.) You send your terrorists to Guantanamo, yes?
CLAIRE	Well, that's not exactly /
ABNER	/ Abu Ghraib. Same difference.
	No nation has the right – let alone moral authority – to lecture us.

CLAIRE   No.

ABNER   In Israel, they're treated properly – as
           prisoners of war.

           They get up in the morning, eat breakfast,
           drink coffee, spend the day in the company
           of their friends. They can even get a college
           degree if they like.

           All courtesy of the Israeli taxpayer.

CLAIRE   Right. But am I correct in saying that nearly
           5,000 Palestinians – including women
           and children – are currently being held in
           administrative detention without charge or
           trial?

ABNER   What you need to understand is that these
           men – and women – are vicious ideologues
           driven by hate and murder. And yet, they
           still receive all their rights and privileges –
           rights and privileges that were denied to the
           families mourning these prisoners' victims.

           The Red Cross, Amnesty, Human Rights
           Watch, B'Tselem – all these human rights
           organisations working day and night to
           improve their conditions.

CLAIRE   Yes, but despite all that, isn't it still the case
           that over 180 children are being held across
           Israeli prisons and detention centres?

ABNER   I don't have the figures to hand.

CLAIRE   But what about the morality of it?
           That kind of power is simply unnatural.

ABNER   You keep painting it in black and white.
           With terrorism there are no morals.
           Politicians prefer binary options – but that
           won't solve the Palestinian question.
           We find ourselves in situations that are
           different shades of gray.

CLAIRE	I've been interviewing a young boy in your prison – only sixteen years old – and it's blindingly clear that he's /
ABNER	/ Careful. You're beginning to conflate matters.
	That young man you speak of may be sixteen years old, but that doesn't make him innocent – he's still a violent threat to our state.
CLAIRE	And I presume you have evidence to support such a charge?
ABNER	Of course – but as you know, I can't share such sensitive and security classified information with you.
	(Beat.) Let's be precise here – call a spade a spade. These terrorists are devoted to their cause.
	(Beat.) And us? What form of questioning must we adopt? *(Beat.)* Civil law procedures which take months for a mere misdemeanor?
	Our success is the undeniable result of the methods we employ. One depends on the other.
	This country made me, and I will express myself as I am – without shame.
	Those who call us fascists forget that our ancestors survived Dachau and Buchenwald. We are soldiers. We were born that way. And our duty is to win.
	So, if I may, let me ask you a question, Claire. *(Beat.)* Should we – Israel – exist in these territories? If your answer is yes, then you must accept all the consequences.
CLAIRE	[…]

LOVER'S ROCK 4

Prison visiting area.

HANEEN is sat waiting. There is a certain bounce – a renewed energy about her.

Pause.

HANEEN checks herself in the screen.

Pause.

SAEED enters – he limps in, badly hurt.

Pause.

SAEED and HANEEN are sat across from one another – separated by a thick glass screen.

HANEEN picks up the receiver.

Pause.

SAEED picks up the receiver.

HANEEN	What happened?
SAEED	It's nothing.
HANEEN	Saeed.
SAEED	I'm fine.
HANEEN	Your face.
SAEED	I promise you – I'm okay.
HANEEN	[…]
SAEED	*(Beat.)* You look well.
HANEEN	[…]

Pause.

SAEED	Haneen.
HANEEN	Yes.
SAEED	What is it?
HANEEN	Nothing. I'm sorry. I was just – *(Beat.)* Thank you. I am – well.
SAEED	That's good.
HANEEN	[…]

SAEED	You know, you don't have to worry about me all the time.
HANEEN	I know.
SAEED	[…]

Pause.

SAEED	Is everything okay?
HANEEN	Yes.
SAEED	[…]
HANEEN	*(Beat.)* We reopened the shop.
SAEED	When?
HANEEN	A couple of weeks ago. We wanted to /
SAEED	/ My bookshop.
HANEEN	Yes.
SAEED	And you decided to do this without talking to me first?
HANEEN	We thought it would make for a nice surprise – some good news. That's all.

Pause.

SAEED	Who's running it?
HANEEN	[…]
SAEED	Well?
HANEEN	*(Beat.)* I am.
SAEED	You?
HANEEN	Yes.
SAEED	How?
HANEEN	What do you mean?
SAEED	How are you running it? *(Beat.)* What about the school?
HANEEN	I quit.
SAEED	What?
HANEEN	I left. I wasn't happy there.

SAEED	But what about the promotion?
	The announcement's in just a couple of months.
HANEEN	I don't want it – I never did.
	I wanted a fresh start.
SAEED	A fresh start? What does that even –
	All the hard work – all that sacrifice. *(Beat.)* For what?
HANEEN	Since when did I need your permission?
	(Beat.) This is my life too, you know.
SAEED	What's going on with you, Haneen?
	I'm stuck in here and everything outside is –
HANEEN	*(Beat.)* Moving on.
SAEED	*(Beat.)* Becoming strange.

Pause.

HANEEN	I can't be dependant on you.
	I need to get on – for both of us.
SAEED	Get on from what?
	I'm still in here.
HANEEN	You say it like I've forgotten – like somehow I don't care.
SAEED	[…]

Pause.

SAEED	If I'm becoming a burden /
HANEEN	/ Stop it.
	That's not what I said.
	(Beat.) I told you, I just feel – smothered.
SAEED	Smothered?
HANEEN	Yes.
SAEED	And what about me? You don't think I'm – smothered – in here?
HANEEN	[…]

SAEED	*(Beat.)* What? You've got nothing more to say?
HANEEN	[…]
SAEED	Fine – get out. *(Beat.)* You can't hurt me, Haneen. No one can hurt me anymore.
HANEEN	If that's what you want.
SAEED	Go – fucking leave. *(Beat.)* Get out – ask them to let you out.

Pause.

SAEED suddenly breaks down – tears come, tears he simply cannot control.

HANEEN	[…]

Pause.

SAEED	Tell me what to do, Haneen. Just tell me. *(Beat.)* I'll do it. I'll be that – I promise you. Tell me what I've got to do. I can't do this – not without you.

Pause.

HANEEN	You act like nothing's wrong. Get on with things. Smile. Laugh even. Eventually you make yourself and everyone else around you believe that it's no longer there – that deadening feeling. *(Beat.)* But it is.
SAEED	[…]
HANEEN	Tell me the truth, Saeed. Tell me something real.

Long pause.

SAEED	Ask me.
HANEEN	[…]
SAEED	Ask me how I am.

	Please.
HANEEN	[…]
SAEED	Please, Haneen. Just –
HANEEN	How are you?
SAEED	[…]
HANEEN	Saeed.
SAEED	*(Beat.)* It doesn't matter.
HANEEN	Saeed. *(Beat.)* Honey.
SAEED	*(Beat.)* I'm not ready.
HANEEN	[…]
SAEED	I'm not ready.
HANEEN	It's okay.
SAEED	I'm not ready.
	I'm just not –
HANEEN	I'm sorry.
SAEED	[…]

Pause.

HANEEN	I'm so sorry about Talal.
SAEED	*(Beat.)* The air's not right in here.
	I can't breathe.

AID COMPLEX

Room.

TOM is sat taking notes.

SHADI	*(Beat.)* Turn it off.
TOM	But we haven't finished yet.
SHADI	I don't care – turn it off.
TOM	[…]
SHADI	Stop recording me, I said.
TOM	Okay. *(Switching off the tape recorder.)* Okay.
SHADI	[…]

TOM   *(Beat.)* We have to release our statement
              tomorrow, Shadi.

              And we still haven't got your testimony
              down yet.

SHADI   [...]

TOM   *(Beat.)* We don't need to record this part.
              So why don't we finish the evaluation?

SHADI   [...]

TOM   *(Looking at his notepad.)* Your cell?

SHADI   [...]

TOM   Your cell, Shadi.

SHADI   Ten.

TOM   Ten?

SHADI   Yeah.

TOM   You know that ten's the best – on our scale.
              From one to ten.

SHADI   Yeah, I know. I'm not an idiot.

TOM   Of course. *(Beat.)* Sorry.

              (Beat.) Okay. So, sanitation.

SHADI   [...]

              Nine – no ten. Yeah, ten.

TOM   [...]

SHADI   [...]

TOM   Food.

SHADI   Hum. Let me think. The chicken's good, real
              good – halal too.

TOM   [...]

SHADI   I'd say then. Yeah, definitely ten.

TOM   Ten – again.

     Pause.

SHADI   Next one.

              (Beat.) Activities?

TOM	*(Beat.)* You think this is a joke?
SHADI	No.
TOM	'Cause I can't do my job if /
SHADI	/ If – if what?

Pause.

TOM	*(Beat.)* We're here to help you.
SHADI	Don't confuse yourself, my friend. You're here to help yourself.
TOM	We're on your side, Shadi. We're doing everything we can to get you out of here. Your detention is in clear violation of the Fourth Geneva Convention.
SHADI	Only because I'm a kid.
TOM	Yes.
SHADI	And if I was a couple years older?
TOM	Well – you're not. That's –
SHADI	If I was Muhib – or Saaed?
TOM	We're doing our best to help everyone, Shadi – each case is different.
SHADI	[…]
TOM	Shadi.
SHADI	What?
TOM	Can we finish up? We really need to get to your testimony.
SHADI	[…]

Pause.

SHADI	*(Beat.)* Why are you here Tom?
TOM	*(Beat.)* Uhm. To help, I guess.
SHADI	But why here? Why Palestine?
TOM	I don't know, Shadi. *(Beat.)* I – I've got an MA in Near and Middle East Studies.

SHADI   […]

TOM   *(Beat.)* My great-granddad's buried here – in the cemetery in Ramleh.

He fought in the First World War.

SHADI   *(Beat.)* Where you from?

TOM   Slough.

SHADI   And what's it like in Slough?

TOM   It's shit mate.

SHADI   So that's why you're here?

TOM   No – not really. *(Beat.)* Maybe.

(Beat.) Can we finish this please?

SHADI   Tell me more about Slough first.

TOM   What do you want to know?

SHADI   I don't know – anything.

TOM   I told you mate. Nothing happens in Slough – it's an utter shit hole.

SHADI   Do people in England like ice cream, Tom?

TOM   Shadi. Please. We have to /

SHADI   / Do you?

Pause.

TOM   *(Beat.)* Yes.

SHADI   My dad works in an ice cream shop in Ramallah.

TOM   Okay.

SHADI   Baldna. *(Beat.)* You know it?

TOM   Yeah.

SHADI   What's your favourite flavour?

TOM   Chocolate – definitely.

(Beat.) And you?

SHADI   I like strawberry.

TOM   Nice. That's a good shout.

SHADI   *(Beat.)* He loved pistachio.

TOM	Who?
SHADI	*(Beat.)* I hung in the air – blood dripping from my body. My shirt covered in blood. My whole body shaking. I remember feeling numb – from the shrapnel that hit me in the thigh.
	We were at this demonstration. My brother, Abed – he was – was standing right next to me. I'd told him not to come, but he wouldn't listen.
	He was hit straight in the head with a tear-gas canister.
TOM	[…]
SHADI	'There is no change nor strength except through Allah, to Allah we belong, and to Him we will return.'
	That's all I remember him saying – my father.

Pause.

TOM	Shadi.
SHADI	[…]
TOM	Shadi. *(Beat.)* Mate – I'm sorry.

Pause.

SHADI	It was sometime in the morning – three – four, maybe. I heard this loud bang – then the sudden stench of gas. There was a flood of soldiers into the house. My mother began shouting, and then I felt someone grab me and rip me out of bed. The soldiers took me outside – to their jeep. My mother followed them – lashing out and screaming. *(Beat.)* But my father – he just stood there – in the doorway. Silent.
	That's the last time I saw them.
TOM	They haven't visited?

SHADI	They're not allowed.
TOM	*(Beat.)* And once you got here?
SHADI	I was undressed and left standing in my underwear. They dragged me for interrogation. They beat me. They beat you hard in those first few days because they know no one's going to see you – or the bruises. And this carried on for days. I don't really know how long. Question after question. I was real hungry – starving. I told them, but they just said I could eat once I'd confessed.
	They put me in this room. It kept going from hot to cold – freezing to boiling. I don't know how they did it. Then, after a few hours, I started to feel my heart beating faster and faster. I shouted for them to let me out. Nothing. I thought my heart was going to explode at any moment.
	A few days later they showed me this video of children throwing stones at soldiers – and – *(Beat.)* And I admitted – that I was one of them. One of the kids in the video.
TOM	[...]
SHADI	It wasn't me though – in the video.
	I just had to – you know.
(Pause.)	
TOM	I know you don't want to, but we have to record this.
SHADI	I told you already.
TOM	Shadi, listen to me. As an advocacy group, our most powerful recourse is to international public opinion. We need to document these horrific incidents.

SHADI	*(Beat.)* And what are you going to do with that testimony, Tom? *(Beat.)* Give it to your superiors?
	(Beat.) And what do you think they're going to do with it?
	(Beat.) You're just wasting your time, my friend.

TIME

ABNER	For activities that threaten regional security.
YAEL / ZIV	Sentence deferred.
Pause.	
SAEED	Six months.

EXERCISE 2

Courtyard.

> *SAEED is jogging steadily in a circle.*
>
> *YAEL is stood still in the centre.*
>
> *Long pause.*
>
> *SAEED begins to pick up the pace.*
>
> *Pause.*

YAEL	Slow down.
Pause.	
YAEL	Hey.
	(Beat.) Slow down.

> *SAEED gradually slows down to a steady pace.*
>
> *Long pause.*

YAEL	Pace yourself – it's not a race.
Long pause.	
YAEL	Cigarette?

SAEED nods his head.

YAEL takes out a packet and holds out a cigarette.

Pause.

SAEED takes the cigarette in his mouth without breaking a stride.

Pause.

YAEL takes out a lighter and holds out the flame.

Pause.

SAEED lights his cigarette without breaking his stride.

SAEED continues jogging and smoking.

Pause.

SAEED picks it up again.

YAEL   Stop running like you're being chased.
           (Beat.) Remember. Pace yourself.

IT'S A BOY

Cell.

SHADI is carrying a cake.

MUHIB's smile is as wide as the ocean.

SHADI starts singing enthusiastically.

SAEED is slightly confused as to the whole affair – he half-joins in.

SHADI hands MUHIB the cake.

MUHIB   *(Taking the cake.)* Kanafeh.

SHADI   Your favourite.

MUHIB   I haven't tasted it in years.

SHADI   Fresh from Al-Aqsa's place in Nablus.

MUHIB   My God. That shop's still going?

SHADI   *(Beat.)* Enjoy it, Muhib.

SAEED   *(To MUHIB.)* What's the occasion?

MUHIB   A grandson.

SAEED	Jibril?
MUHIB	[...]
SAEED	*(Beat.)* What's that now? *(Beat.)* Six?
MUHIB	No. Yusuf.
SAEED	Yusuf?
MUHIB	It's his first.
SAEED	[...]
MUHIB	A boy too.
SAEED	But Yusuf's been in prison for over a year now?
MUHIB	Eighteen months.

SAEED laughs.

MUHIB	*(Smiling.)* Yes, a miracle, my son.
SAEED	*(Beat.)* So what are we celebrating?
MUHIB	[...]
SAEED	[...]
MUHIB	I told you. *(Beat.)* Fadi – Yusuf's son.
SAEED	But that doesn't make any sense.
	(Beat.) Come on. Stop messing me around Muhib. What is this all about?
SHADI	Give me a piece.
MUHIB	Get out of here.
SHADI	Come on – I'm fucking hungry.
MUHIB	This one's mine – all mine.
	[...]
SHADI	Go on.
MUHIB	[...]
SHADI	Muhib.
MUHIB	Yes.
SHADI	Take a bite.
MUHIB	Yeah.

Pause.

MUHIB takes a bite of the cake.

Pause.

SHADI	*(Giving MUHIB a kiss.)* Congratulations brother.
	May God bless him and give him strength in both your absences.
SAEED	[…]
SHADI	Saeed.
SAEED	Yes.
SHADI	Aren't you going to –
SAEED	*(Beat.)* Yeah. Of course.

Pause.

SAEED	*(Hugging and embracing MUHIB.)* Come here. Congratulations.
	May God look over them both.
MUHIB	Thank you.
	Both of us should be thanking you.
SHADI	Why did you do it?
	They wouldn't have done anything to Muhib.
SAEED	[…]
MUHIB	I understand why.
SAEED	I'm not a traitor.
MUHIB	We know that, son.
SAEED	*(Beat.)* What happened to Akram?
SHADI	[…]
MUHIB	[…]
SHADI	He died – killed himself.
SAEED	I'm sorry. I didn't mean – last time.
MUHIB	Sixty-four years old, he was. Fit as an ox.
	We shared a cell for over fourteen years.
	(Beat.) Hung himself with his sheets.

	He couldn't take it anymore – just gave up.
SAEED	[...]
SHADI	Come on guys.
	Pause.
SHADI	*(Beat.)* Come on. It's a great day. *(Beat.)* Let's celebrate.
MUHIB	Wait. *(Beat.)* Before that. Give me those pills they gave you.
SAEED	What pills?
MUHIB	Come on, Saeed. *(Beat.)* Give them to me.
SAEED	I can't.
MUHIB	Saaed.
SAEED	I need them.
MUHIB	No, you don't.
SAEED	For my heart. My heart isn't –
MUHIB	There's nothing wrong with you, Saaed.
SAEED	I'm not losing my mind.
MUHIB	You're not the only one they give it to. They're just fucking with you. *(Beat.)* Now, come on – give them to me.
SAEED	[...]
MUHIB	You don't need them. Trust me, Saeed.

Pause.

SAEED takes out the bottle of pills and slowly hands them over to MUHIB.

MUHIB takes the bottle and quickly empties its contents on the floor. He then starts crushing the pills with his shoe.

| SAEED | No.
Muhib – no. |

SAEED falls to his knees and tries to collect the pills.

MUHIB	It's for the best, Saaed.
SAEED	No. No.
	What have you done?
MUHIB	Stop, Saeed. *(Beat.)* Just stop.
	(Beat.) Look at you – look at what they've done to you.

Pause.

SAEED	*(Holding some cracked pills.)* […]

Pause.

MUHIB	Get up.
SAEED	[…]
MUHIB	Come on, Saeed.

MUHIB and SHADI both help SAEED up and sit him down on one of the beds.

MUHIB takes out a packet of cigarettes and lights one.

MUHIB takes a toke and then hands the cigarette to SAEED.

SAEED	[…]
MUHIB	Take.

SAEED takes the cigarette.

MUHIB lights another one.

Pause.

MUHIB	Tall, he was. Imposing. He had these piercing eyes.
	We shared a cell for five years.
SAEED	Who?
MUHIB	I knew him.

BACK TO THE START

1990.

Prison visiting area.

KHALIL and ASMA are sat across from one another.

KHALIL's broken arm is in a crude sling.

ASMA is wearing a beautiful floral dress.
Pause.

KHALIL	It's nothing.
ASMA	[…]

    ASMA takes KHALIL's arm.

    KHALIL winces sharply – and recoils.

ASMA	*(Beat.)* Nothing, is it?
KHALIL	You should see the guard – the state I left him in.
ASMA	You stubborn fool.
KHALIL	He won't be pulling that shit on any one of us again.
ASMA	No, but the next one will – and then the one after that.
KHALIL	What's been the response?
ASMA	It's being called a confidence-building measure.
KHALIL	Rubbish – it's just another smokescreen.
ASMA	There's rumours of a multi-party conference in Madrid to try and open up new negotiating tracks.
	They say it might even lay the groundwork for an interim agreement.
KHALIL	With everything else going on at the moment?
	(Beat.) I don't like it.

ASMA   The American Secretary of State's already
        made a number of trips.
        (Beat.) It's all part of the game – we've got to
        play it.

KHALIL They won't let us in.
        (Beat.) What's Ahmed saying?

ASMA   He's thinking of signing.

KHALIL There's no such thing as goodwill gestures
        – confidence-building. It always comes at a
        price.

ASMA   You'll be released in stages.

KHALIL So we've already agreed terms?

ASMA   Not yet.
        Yitzhak Shamir wants to announce it in the
        next two weeks – spin it to public – try and
        turn it into some kind of moral victory.

KHALIL How many?

ASMA   We don't know yet.

KHALIL Tell Ahmed to leave me to the final group –
        make sure the others get out.
        You know how these sons of bitches are.

ASMA   [...]

KHALIL *(Taking ASMA's hand.)* Hey. Hey.
        I'll be out of here soon enough.

ASMA   *(Beat.)* Saeed's been asking about you – he
        misses you.

KHALIL Asma. We agreed not to tell them anything.

ASMA   I know.
        I just don't think he'll believe /

KHALIL / Asma. *(Beat.)* Listen to me.
        Saeed and Talal shouldn't have to deal with
        any of this.

ASMA   [...]

KHALIL Honey.

ASMA	Yes.
KHALIL	What's wrong?
ASMA	We can't just keep it from them forever.
KHALIL	I know. But now isn't the right time – not while I'm still in here.
	I want to be able to explain it to them myself.
ASMA	[…]
KHALIL	I'm going to make things right.
	Once this is all over, we'll be able to live our lives.
ASMA	We're already doing the right thing.
KHALIL	I know. But this – this isn't –
ASMA	This is what we stand for. We have to remain steadfast.
KHALIL	[…]

Pause.

ASMA	I visited Muhammad yesterday.
KHALIL	How is he?
ASMA	He's staying positive.
KHALIL	How bad is it?
ASMA	They don't know yet.
KHALIL	Who's with him?
ASMA	Fatima.
KHALIL	I don't want my father to be alone there.
ASMA	He won't be – we're all there for him.

Pause.

ASMA	I brought your favourite.
KHALIL	Baklava?

ASMA nods.

KHALIL	From Abu Nassi's?

ASMA takes out a small packet of sweets.

KHALIL   *(Smiling.)* I love you.

ASMA   You should – the trouble I had to go through.

KHALIL   *(Beat.)* Feed one to me.

ASMA   […]

KHALIL   Go on.

ASMA   *(Beat.)* Open your mouth.

KHALIL opens his mouth.

ASMA gently feeds him a piece.

Pause.

ASMA smiles.

KHALIL   That tastes so good.

Pause.

ASMA   It's time.

KHALIL   Okay.

ASMA   It's from Ahmed.

KHALIL nods.

Pause.

ASMA   It's going to be alright.

KHALIL   Yeah.

ASMA   I love you.

KHALIL   […]

ASMA and KHALIL embrace – passing a note on through mouth-to-mouth.

Pause.

KHALIL nods.

ASMA exits.

INSTRUCTIONS

1990.

Cell.

KHALIL's gagging.

Pause.

KHALIL's gagging.

Pause.

KHALIL coughs up a tightly rolled piece of cigarette paper.

Pause.

KHALIL unfurls the piece of paper and starts to read it.

MUHIB	So?
KHALIL	[…]
MUHIB	*(Beat.)* What does it say?
KHALIL	Wait.
MUHIB	Have we agreed?

Pause.

KHALIL	Ahmed's decided to sign.
MUHIB	And the release?
KHALIL	Yes.
MUHIB	How many?
KHALIL	It doesn't say.
MUHIB	What does it say?
KHALIL	The first group will be released from here next Friday.
MUHIB	Who?
KHALIL	[…]
MUHIB	Khalil.

Pause.

KHALIL smiles and nods his head.

MUHIB	Yes?

KHALIL	Yeah.

KHALIL and MUHIB hug – hard.

MUHIB	I thought it'll never come.
KHALIL	So you going to tell Afaf?
MUHIB	You must be crazy. Getting away from her was the one saving grace of being in this shit hole.
KHALIL	You know she'll be there when you get out – right there – standing by the gates.
MUHIB	Shit – if she is, I'll beg the guards to take me straight back in.
KHALIL	She's a good woman – Afaf.

Pause.

MUHIB	*(Beat.)* You going to be alright?
KHALIL	I'll be fine. One of us needs to stay – look out for the others.
MUHIB	When it's all over, we'll take the kids to Rafidiyah – eat kofta – look over the city.
KHALIL	I'd like that.

Pause.

KHALIL	*(Beat.)* Come on. We should celebrate.

KHALIL takes out a lighter and burns the piece of paper.

LOVERS ROCK 5

Prison visiting area.

SAEED and HANEEN are sat across from one another – separated by a thick glass screen.

SAEED is smiling profusely.

SAEED picks up the receiver.

HANEEN picks up the receiver.

SAEED	[…]

HANEEN	Why are you smiling?
SAEED	[…]
HANEEN	What is it?
SAEED	[…]
HANEEN	*(Beat.)* Stop it.
SAEED	Listen to me.
HANEEN	What?
SAEED	Will you listen?
HANEEN	Yes. Tell me.
SAEED	*(Beat.)* Okay –
HANEEN	Saeed? *(Beat.)* What /
SAEED	/ I want to try again.
HANEEN	[…]
SAEED	I want us to – again.

Pause.

HANEEN	Saeed /
SAEED	I'm not going mad. Believe me. *(Beat.)* What if /
HANEEN	Saeed /
SAEED	/ Haneen. Listen to me – just listen.
SAEED	There's a way we can do it.
HANEEN	[…]
SAEED	Yusuf's in prison and he just had his first child – a son. Fadi.
HANEEN	What are you talking about, Saeed?
SAEED	I'm trying to tell you that we can still do this.
HANEEN	Do what?
SAEED	There's people in here who can help us – help me smuggle it out.
HANEEN	Stop, Saeed. Just stop.
SAEED	[…]

HANEEN   You've absolutely lost it – lost your fucking mind.

I don't want to hear any more of this.

SAEED   Just listen to me, Haneen.

HANEEN   No. Yusuf's not my husband – and Fadi's not my child.

Do you hear me?

SAEED   […]

HANEEN   *(Beat.)* And what if I don't want to – while you're in here.

Did you even –

Did you at any point think about what I might want?

(Beat.) Have you forgotten already?

SAEED   […]

HANEEN   Because I haven't.

We even named him – as he kicked – before –

(Beat.) Do you remember?

SAEED   […]

HANEEN   *(Beat.)* Do you, Saeed?

SAEED   This isn't just about you, Haneen.

(Beat.) We need to move on.

HANEEN   You selfish bastard.

SAEED   You're my wife.

HANEEN   How dare you.

After everything we've been through.

(Beat.) You think these visits are easy for me?

Coming here – having these fucking guards humiliating me, touching me.

(Beat.) And for what?

All to see you – like this?

Pause.

SAEED   *(Beat.)* I'm sorry. I didn't mean –

HANEEN	Why are you doing this?
SAEED	I need something, Haneen.
	I really need something – something real – something that's ours.
HANEEN	[…]
SAEED	I don't know how long I'm going to be here. They keep extending my –
	What if I'm here for /
HANEEN	/ Saeed.
SAEED	We need to show them – show them all. Defy them.
HANEEN	This isn't you talking.
SAEED	It is.
HANEEN	[…]
SAEED	I was born into this life. They won't take that away from me.
	We will bring life into our home.
	We will defeat them with our hope – our resilience.
HANEEN	[…]
SAEED	*(Beat.)* I'm afraid, Haneen.
	We're not the same – my father and I.
	I don't want to make the same mistakes he did.
HANEEN	You won't.

Pause.

HANEEN	You really want this?
SAEED	I really want us to do this – together.
HANEEN	I need to know that you want it for the right reasons, Saeed – for us.
SAEED	I want us to be a family again.
	And I know you want that as much as I do.
HANEEN	[…]

Pause.

SAEED   Rasul. *(Beat.)* Our son's name was Rasul.

A FATHER'S SON

1990.

Cell.

The faint sound of the Adhan [Islamic call to prayer] can be made out.

Pause.

KHALIL prostrates and performs morning prayers.

Pause.

The Adhan is followed by a roll call of those recently deceased.

Pause.

The name Muhammad Shaka is called out.

KHALIL   […]

   Pause.

                   Guard.

   Pause.

                   Guard.

   Pause.

                   (Rattling the bars.) (Beat.) Hey. Guard. *(Beat.)*
                   Hey.
                   Let me out.
                   (Beat.) Son of a bitch. *(Beat.)* Hey.

   Pause.

                   I want to see him.
                   I want to see my father.
                   I have the right to –

KHALIL suddenly slumps to the floor.

   Pause.

                   Please. Just let –

I only want to see him.

Pause.

[...]

KHALIL suddenly erupts in a fit of rage, destroying his cell in the process – the bed, chair, table – anything and everything in sight.

A DEAL'S A DEAL

Cell.

SHADI is fast asleep.

SAEED	The sleep of innocence.
MUHIB	It's the whisky that's sleeping.
SAEED	I don't miss it – my innocence.
MUHIB	Whisky's more truthful than water. Tells you who's real and who isn't.
SAEED	You're one of those men – drinks his weaponry and wakes up speaking swords.
MUHIB	You're probably right.
	Your father was such a man – we all were back then.
	It's not the same anymore though.

Pause.

SAEED	Muhib.
MUHIB	Yeah.
SAEED	I need your help.
MUHIB	Go on.
SAEED	Yusuf.
MUHIB	What about him?
SAEED	I know how it works.
MUHIB	You do, do you?
SAEED	I've asked around – I know you set it up, Muhib.
MUHIB	You need to feel alive – I understand.

SAEED	[…]
MUHIB	You're living, see, but it's all a bit flat. A bit flawless.
	You need a cause. It's part of our condition.
	(Beat.) But I can't help you with this – there's too much risk involved.
SAEED	Too much risk? We're in fucking prison. What more /
MUHIB	/ I'm sorry, Saaed.
SAEED	[…]
MUHIB	*(Beat.)* You want anything else – plasma TV, better phone, drugs – I can sort you out. But this – I just can't.
SAEED	But what about Yusuf?
MUHIB	Yusuf's my son.
	His new son is my grandchild.
	(Beat.) Do you understand the difference?
SAEED	[…]

Pause.

SAEED	Fuck you.
MUHIB	*(Laughing.)* I'll let you have that one.
	(Beat.) You're upset – I can see that.
SAEED	*(Pushing MUHIB up against the wall.)* I know your dirty little game.
	I've spent my whole life trying to avoid men like you. The type who peddles in the filthiest of markets – ruining other people's dreams.
MUHIB	*(Smiling.)* You got me.
SAEED	[…]
MUHIB	You got me.

Pause.

MUHIB	Now, let go.

Come on. *(Beat.)* It's alright.

SAEED slowly lets go of MUHIB.

	A man – finally.
	It took you a while.
SAEED	I'm sorry. I didn't –
MUHIB	I'm proud of you son.
SAEED	[…]
MUHIB	Come on.
SAEED	Yeah.
MUHIB	Good.

Pause.

	(Grabbing SAEED by the neck.) It seems like you're no longer scared of me.
	(Beat.) Huh?
SAEED	*(Struggling.)* Let go –
MUHIB	Is that true?
SAEED	*(Struggling.)* Let go of me. *(Beat.)* Please.

MUHIB throws SAEED to the ground.

MUHIB	If you can walk around here freely, it's because of me.
SAEED	[…]
MUHIB	If you live, think, it's thanks to me.
SAEED	[…]
MUHIB	You live off me.
SAEED	[…]
MUHIB	Do you hear me?
SAEED	*(Beat.)* Yes.
MUHIB	Good.

Pause.

MUHIB	Get up.
SAEED	[…]

MUHIB   Get up, I said.

SAEED pulls himself up.

Pause.

SAEED   *(Whispering.) (Beat.)* I need this.

MUHIB   What? *(Beat.)* What do you need?

SAEED   I need this.

MUHIB   No – you need me.

SAEED   Please.

Pause.

MUHIB   Okay.

                     (Beat.) But you're going to have to do
                     something for me.

SAEED   […]

MUHIB dusts SAEED down.

MUHIB   Sit down.

                     (Beat.) Go on. *(Beat.)* Sit.

SAEED sits down.

                     They've called for a day of rage across all the
                     prisons on Friday.

SAEED   And what do you want from me?

*MUHIB goes to SHADI's bed and carefully removes a small wrapped
towel from underneath the bed frame.*

MUHIB   When the guards come in to lock us down,
                     you're going to take one of them out.

SAEED   What?

MUHIB starts unwrapping the towel.

MUHIB   They'll put us against the wall as usual.
                     They'll check me first – the same routine.
                     And that's your chance – your moment to
                     strike whoever's searching me.

SAEED   No – I can't.

MUHIB   Do you want people to listen to you, Saaed?

SAEED	[…]
MUHIB	Well?
SAEED	Of course I do – but this is crazy.
MUHIB	*(Revealing a makeshift knife.)* You think you can be in this world and not part of it?
	That privilege doesn't exist for people like us.
	You're here because of who you are – and that's something you'll never be able to change.
SAEED	[…]
MUHIB	There are men of words – men of capital – but what has happened to men of actions, Saeed?
	We're those spirited men – in here.
SAEED	I'll go for life.
MUHIB	Nothing in this world comes for free – nothing meaningful.
SAEED	[…]
MUHIB	Listen. I'm not here to bargain with you, Saaed.
SAEED	But what if /
MUHIB	/ It's never a good thing to reject a friendly offer.
SAEED	[…]
MUHIB	Do you understand?

MUHIB extends the towel to SAEED.

SAEED	[…]
MUHIB	Make your decision.
	(Beat.) You know what you have to do.
SAEED	[…]

A CHANGE OF HEART

1990.
Prison visiting area.

Not clear this was earlier.

KHALIL and ASMA are sat across from one another.
Pause.
ASMA hands KHALIL a gold pendant.
Pause.

ASMA   Your father wanted you to have it.

   KHALIL takes the pendant.

   Pause.

KHALIL   Was he in pain?

ASMA   No. He went in his sleep.
                It was peaceful.

KHALIL   He wasn't alone?

ASMA   We were all there with him.

KHALIL   *(Beat.)* And the funeral?

ASMA   Fatima and I organised it.
                We buried him in Awarta – next to Mustafa
                and Fuad.

KHALIL   He should be with my mother.
                He should be at home – in Jaffa – with his
                mother and father.

ASMA   […]

KHALIL   And where was Ahmed?
                He should have organised it all.

ASMA   *(Beat.)* Khalil.

KHALIL   What?

ASMA   Ahmed's been arrested.

KHALIL   When?

ASMA   Two nights ago.

KHALIL   How?

ASMA	They raided us – swamped the old city. The offices – the arms cache – our printing machines. All of it. Everything.
KHALIL	Did they get to our house?
ASMA	No. *(Beat.)* They didn't even bother. They knew exactly where to go. They searched and found everything.
KHALIL	And where's Ahmed now?
ASMA	They've got him in administrative detention. They're planning to exile him to Jordan. They demolished their home.
KHALIL	[…]
ASMA	Hala and the children are staying with us.
KHALIL	Asma. *(Beat.)* We agreed not to blur matters.
ASMA	They've got nowhere else to go.
KHALIL	*(Beat.)* Who's in charge now?
ASMA	Farouk.
KHALIL	His brother-in-law. *(Beat.)* Of course. He's a boy.
ASMA	Khalil. This isn't –
KHALIL	What?
ASMA	They've called for a day of rage in all the prisons.
KHALIL	Who's they? *(Beat.)* You mean Farouk has? Of course – what would Farouk know about –
ASMA	Why are you being like this?
KHALIL	[…]

Pause.

KHALIL	And what about the exchange?
ASMA	It's still on – as planned. The first group will be released on Friday.
KHALIL	[…]

Pause.

ASMA	It's time.
KHALIL	[…]
ASMA	It's from Farouk.
KHALIL	[…]
ASMA	Khalil.
KHALIL	Yeah.
ASMA	From Farouk.

Pause.

ASMA leans in to kiss KHALIL – to pass on a note.

KHALIL	[…]
ASMA	*(Still half-leaning in.)* Khalil.
KHALIL	[…]
ASMA	*(Sitting back.)* Khalil.
	What are you doing?
	(Beat.) Take it.
KHALIL	[…]
ASMA	Say something.
KHALIL	I can't.
ASMA	Not now, Khalil.
	(Beat.) Take it.
KHALIL	You're asking me to do something – be something I'm not.
	(Beat.) I can't – not anymore.
ASMA	Khalil. This isn't the time.
	We need you to remain focused – now more than ever.
KHALIL	This game of heroes and cowards – I'm tired of it.
	I know what courage is. And this isn't it.
ASMA	You're dealing with a lot right now. You just need to clear your head.

	Think about everything we have to live for.
KHALIL	I am.
	All I want is to lay my head on your stomach. Share a cigarette. Have Saeed and Talal playing at our feet. Laughing – I want to hear their laughter.
ASMA	[…]
KHALIL	I'm done with the movement, Asma. I'm out – for good.
ASMA	Khalil. You can't do this.
	Take the note.
KHALIL	I won't.
ASMA	Khalil. Please.
KHALIL	*(Beat.)* Tell Farouk I'm leaving in the first group.

KHALIL exits.

| ASMA | You can't just – *(Beat.)* Khalil. |

Pause.

ASMA exits.

ALL FOR THE CAUSE

Cell.

MUHIB is fast asleep.

KHALIL is watching MUHIB.

Pause.

KHALIL takes out a pen and piece of scrap cigarette paper.

KHALIL stares at MUHIB – quickly scribbling something down.

KHALIL puts the pen away and neatly rolls up the note.

KHALIL takes the note in his mouth.

Long pause.

KHALIL watches MUHIB sleep.

Pause.

KHALIL's gagging.

Pause.

KHALIL's gagging.

MUHIB   *(Rubbing his face.)* What is it?

   KHALIL's gagging.

MUHIB   *(Getting up.)* You alright?

   KHALIL coughs up the tightly rolled up note.

   Pause.

   KHALIL unfurls the piece of paper and starts to read it.

MUHIB   What is it?

KHALIL   […]

MUHIB   What?

KHALIL   Wait.

MUHIB   I thought we were set for Friday.

KHALIL   They've got Ahmed.

MUHIB   What do you mean?

KHALIL   He's been arrested.

MUHIB   *(Beat.)* Fuck.

KHALIL   They raided the old city two nights ago – our offices, everything.

MUHIB   […]

KHALIL   They found it all.

               (Beat.) Shit.

MUHIB   What about the release?

   Pause.

KHALIL   It's still going ahead.

MUHIB   Okay.

KHALIL   Muhib.

MUHIB   We need to reorganise.

KHALIL	Muhib.
MUHIB	Strike those sons of bitches back – hard.
KHALIL	Muhib.
	Listen to me.
MUHIB	What?
KHALIL	[...]
MUHIB	What is it?
KHALIL	There's been a change of plan.
MUHIB	What do you mean?
KHALIL	[...]
MUHIB	What is it?
KHALIL	They need me.
MUHIB	I don't understand.
KHALIL	They need me to help pick up the pieces – rebuild.
MUHIB	And?
KHALIL	*(Beat.)* You're not going – not in the first group.
MUHIB	Come on.
	You're joking, right?
KHALIL	[...]
MUHIB	Khalil.
KHALIL	[...]
MUHIB	Khalil.
KHALIL	[...]
MUHIB	Say something, Khalil.
	Fucking say something.
	You /
KHALIL	/ Careful.
MUHIB	[...]

Pause.

MUHIB	*(Beat.)* On whose order?

KHALIL	Farouk.
MUHIB	Farouk.
	Farouk – Ahmed's brother-in-law?
KHALIL	Yeah.
MUHIB	Farouk's in charge now, is he?
KHALIL	For the moment, yes.
MUHIB	Let me see.
KHALIL	[…]
MUHIB	Give me that.

KHALIL hands the piece of paper over to MUHIB.

MUHIB	*(Reading the note.)* […]

Pause.

MUHIB	*(Beat.)* Motherfuckers.
KHALIL	[…]
MUHIB	This is bullshit.
	You wouldn't fucking /
KHALIL	/ Hey. *(Beat.)* Remember who you're talking to.
MUHIB	[…]
KHALIL	*(Beat.)* Listen. It's not personal, Muhib.
MUHIB	What am I going to tell Afaf?
KHALIL	She'll understand.
MUHIB	[…]
KHALIL	*(Beat.)* Hey
	Stay strong.

Pause.

MUHIB rolls himself a smoke.

Pause.

MUHIB	I was dreaming.
KHALIL	When?
MUHIB	Just now – before you woke me.

KHALIL	Afaf?
	(Beat.) Who was on top?
MUHIB	*(Beat.)* No.
KHALIL	[…]
MUHIB	*(Beat.)* You were there though.
KHALIL	[…]

MUHIB burns the piece of paper with his rollie.

THERE'S A RIOT GOIN' ON

Cell.

The rising sound of a prison increasingly losing any sense of order – the day of rage has arrived.

PRISONERS	*(Offstage.)* Courage my brothers! Courage!

MUHIB, SHADI & SAEED are on a rampage – shouting, hollering and turning their cell upside down.

PRISONERS	*(Offstage.)* Courage my brothers! Courage!

ABNER, YAEL and ZIV rush in.

PRISONERS	*(Offstage.)* Courage my brothers! Courage!

MUHIB and SAEED move to the wall.

ABNER	Shadi.
SHADI	Fuck off.
ABNER	That mouth of yours – it'll get you in trouble.
	(Beat.) Now I'm not going to say it again – against the fucking wall.

Pause.

SHADI stands his ground.

ABNER strikes SHADI with a heavy blow.

Pause.

ABNER	*(To YAEL.)* Check them.
YAEL	*(To MUHIB.)* Hands on your head.

MUHIB raises his hands.

YAEL starts searching MUHIB.

Pause.

SHADI stands his ground.

YAEL   Spread your legs.

MUHIB spreads his legs.

MUHIB looks over to SAEED.

Pause.

ABNER strikes SHADI with another heavy blow.

SHADI falls to his knees and spits blood.

ABNER   Is it worth it? *(Beat.)* Your insolence.

SAEED reaches into his pocket – he hesitates and keeps his hand there.

MUHIB looks over again at SAEED.

Pause.

YAEL   Okay.

MUHIB   […]

ABNER notices that SHADI has just wet himself.

ABNER   Look at you – it's fucking disgusting.

YAEL   *(To SAEED.)* Hands on your head.

SAEED   […]

YAEL   Hands on your head, I said.

MUHIB   […]

SAEED takes his hand out of his pocket – clenching the makeshift knife – and raises his hands.

Pause.

SAEED grips the makeshift knife and stabs ABNER.

ABNER falls to the ground bleeding.

The alarm is sounded.

SAEED   Fuck. *(Beat.)* What have I –

SAEED drops the knife – shocked at his act.

SAEED   No – look at what I've done.

ZIV attacks SAEED.

Tear gas is pumped through the vent.

In the resulting mêlée, riot police flood the cell.

ZIV starts to break down as he continues to beat SAEED to a pulp.

Pause.

YAEL slowly undresses. She then removes ABNER's Captain's uniform and puts it on.

YAEL   People should see when they've been
               mastered. If they don't, then our duty
               is to remind them – constantly.
               We can't allow them to think that the status
               quo can be seized.
               We have a responsibility to reconstitute this
               world.
               (To ZIV.) (Beat.) Take him out.

SAEED eventually emerges – he is handcuffed and shackled.

Pause.

MUHIB   You're finally free, Saeed – a man no longer
               possessed by his father's shadow.

SAEED   But I'm all on my own.

MUHIB   Not at all.
               You're one of us now, son.

TIME

YAEL   One count of first-degree murder.

ZIV   Two life sentences.

EXERCISE 3

Courtyard.

SAEED is jogging steadily in a circle.

ZIV is stood still in the centre.

Long pause.

SAEED begins to pick up the pace.

Pause.

ZIV   Slow down.

    Pause.

                Slow down, I said.

                Pace yourself – it's not a race.

SAEED gradually slows down to a steady pace.

Long pause.

                Do you know how long you're in for?

Pause.

                A while.

Pause.

                A very long while.

SAEED picks it up again.

Pause.

                Stop running like you're being chased.

                (Beat.) Remember. Pace yourself.

Long pause.

                Let me give you a piece of solid advice.

                (Beat.) Let go of the past. Forget it.

                The past is dead, Saeed.

A FAMILY AFFAIR

Prison visiting area.

SAEED and KHALIL are sat across from one another – separated by a thick glass screen.

Pause.

KHALIL picks up the receiver.

Pause.

KHALIL   [...]

Pause.

SAEED picks up the receiver.

Pause.

KHALIL	How are you, son?
SAEED	[...]
KHALIL	Well, Haneen's well – glowing actually.
SAEED	[...]
KHALIL	She's kicking – a lot.
SAEED	[...]
KHALIL	You want to see a photo?
SAEED	[...]
KHALIL	You should see –

KHALIL takes out a photo from his jacket pocket.

KHALIL	*(Gently placing the photo against the glass screen.)* Look son.
SAEED	[...]
KHALIL	Look at how happy she is.

Pause.

SAEED   *(Beat.)* Take it away.

Pause.

KHALIL takes down the photo.

Pause.

KHALIL   *(Beat.)* Listen to me.
I didn't wish for this.
I didn't want things to end up like –

Pause.

SAEED   *(Beat.)* Why are you here?

KHALIL   What do you mean?
You're my son.

SAEED   What do you want?

KHALIL   Nothing.

SAEED   […]

KHALIL   Saeed, son. Listen to me.
(Beat.) I'm sorry –
I'm sorry I haven't been there.
I should have visited, but I –

SAEED   But we're bad for business – my dead
brother and I. Ruin your sweet deal,
would we?

KHALIL   That's not true.

SAEED   Why did you never tell us?

KHALIL   *(Beat.)* About what?

SAEED   Your past.

KHALIL   What are you talking about?

SAEED   The Night of the Gliders.

KHALIL   […]

SAEED   Ktzi'ot Prison.

KHALIL   […]

SAEED   I know all about it.

KHALIL   […]

SAEED   *(Beat.)* Your face.
Your face right now. It's a picture – I wish
you could see it.

Pause.

KHALIL	How do you know about that?
SAEED	Why didn't you tell us?
KHALIL	Because you didn't need to know.
SAEED	[...]
KHALIL	*(Beat.)* Who told you?
SAEED	Muhib Samaha.
KHALIL	Muhib Samaha. *(Beat.)* And how do you know Muhib?
SAEED	He was my cellmate.
KHALIL	[...]
SAEED	That's right.
KHALIL	And you believe him? *(Beat.)* That man's full of shit.
SAEED	He is. But not as much as you, father.
KHALIL	I was trying to protect you – all of you.
SAEED	From what?
KHALIL	From a similar fate to mine. I didn't want you to end up –
SAEED	What? *(Beat.)* Like this? One in here and the other dead – murdered.
KHALIL	I'm your damn father. *(Beat.)* All I ever wanted was to build a home for you all.
SAEED	*(Beat.)* And what about mother?
KHALIL	Asma was with me.
SAEED	You're lying. Who is it that you're loyal to, father?
KHALIL	You know nothing. *(Beat.)* Your mother – she sacrificed everything.

135

	I loved her. More than you'll ever know.
	I loved you and your brother.
SAEED	And now you build another lie – a monster on our hills – some pus-filled sore, and feed it to the people like cake.
KHALIL	You ungrateful –
	One day you'll realise who I did all this for.
	(Beat.) How do you think anyone manages to wrestle control over their own destiny? *(Beat.)* Huh?
	(Beat.) You think it's given? *(Beat.)* That you're born with it?
	If you do, then you've learnt nothing, my son.
	You have to grab it. Grab it by the neck – its life in your hands – and name it.
	That's the only way to claim anything in this world.
SAEED	You're poison.
	You're just a lowly comprador – a native servant. You're not building our dreams – you're manufacturing foreign fantasies.
	And I tell you, they won't survive.
KHALIL	You're lost. Stuck.
	It's time for us to live our lives.
SAEED	However much you try, you won't be able to deny our history – our struggle.
KHALIL	You really think that's what I'm doing?
SAEED	You can't just simply wash everything away with this mad delusion of yours.

Pause.

KHALIL	*(Beat.)* I've got them a new place there.
SAEED	[…]
KHALIL	On a clear day they'll be able to see the Mediterranean from their terrace.

SAEED	They may be able to see, but feel it, they won't. They'll still have to dream about dipping their toes in that clear, warm water.
KHALIL	Haneen will move in once the baby's born.
SAEED	No they won't. They're –
KHALIL	What's done is done, Saeed.
SAEED	No, you won't – not on my –
KHALIL	Saeed. *(Beat.)* Listen to me.
	We have the right to ambition – to not feel guilty for wanting better for our families.
SAEED	I hate you. I hate everything you represent.
KHALIL	Mind your mouth.
	I'm sick of children playing revolution – I made hard choices.
	I will live and move on. My grandchildren will live for themselves – for their generation. They won't be held back by our mistakes anymore.
	Nothing is worth dying for – one day you'll see.
SAEED	I want you to stay away from my family.
KHALIL	[...]
SAEED	Do you hear me, father?
KHALIL	I'm just looking after them – for you.
SAEED	You couldn't even do that for your own children.
KHALIL	[...]
SAEED	I'm warning you.
	Stay away from them.

SAEED exits.

KHALIL is left alone – full of his own thoughts.

A HAPPY ENDING (OF SORTS)

SAEED and HANEEN in parallel worlds.
HANEEN is seven months pregnant.

HANEEN   Stop it – that tickles.

    SAEED smiles.

HANEEN   *(Rubbing her belly.)* Stop it.

    SAEED smiles.

    Pause.

SAEED   I want to tell you about the future.
              I'm an old man.

HANEEN   Who are you talking to?

SAEED   Shhh.
              (Beat.) Not you – I'm talking to her. *(Beat.)*
              Our little one.

    HANEEN smiles.

SAEED   I'm an old man. We're standing by the sea –
              I hold your hand.
              You're a woman now.

    Pause.

SAEED   When I die – when I die I will be by the sea.

    Pause.

SAEED   This plan was never based on a dream. It
              was formulated in reality – in this world.
              Between these concrete walls.
              I wanted nothing else than to grow old, sit in
              a rocking chair, see my grandchildren play
              by my feet.
              (Beat.) But that was never going to happen,
              was it? That was the fantasy – the one I saw
              in my dreams.

So I'll Ieave you the pleasure of telling that story.

Blackout.

The End.

BY THE SAME AUTHOR

Sour Lips
9781849434768

I was still living as an Arab Muslim in America. I struggled with coming out to friends and family, and so I decided to come back to Syria. It hasn't been easy. But we are here, just as we are everywhere.

DAMASCUS 18:00 – Amina was walking near Fares Al-Khouri Street when three armed men seized her. According to an eyewitness, Amina was bustled into a red Dacia Logan with a bumper sticker of Basel Assad. The men are assumed to be members of the Ba'ath Partymilitia or one of the security services. Amina's present location is still unknown. Following the story of Amina Arraf, the blogger known as 'A Gay Girl In Damascus', and the events fomented by the media's coverage of her kidnapping, *Sour Lips* fuses fantasy and non-fiction to create its own speculative narrative.

WWW.OBERONBOOKS.COM

 Follow us on www.twitter.com/@oberonbooks
& www.facebook.com/oberonbook